HERITAGE CRAFTS TODAY

Glass Beads

0 11557 00376 5

Glass Beads

Tips, Tools, and Techniques for Learning the Craft

LOUISE MEHAFFEY

Photography by Kevin Brett

STACKPOLE
BOOKS

To my husband and children,
who have tolerated my obsession with glass for many years,
and to my glass tribe

Published by
STACKPOLE BOOKS
5067 Ritter Road
Mechanicsburg, PA 17055
www.stackpolebooks.com

Warning

Making glass beads is a dangerous process that requires using glass materials and hazardous gases and flames. Although safety precautions are noted throughout this book, they are not meant as substitutes for common sense and caution. All persons following the steps for making the glass beads in this book do so at their own risk. The author and publisher disclaim any and all liability for any injuries that may result from the execution of the steps provided here.

Printed in China

10 9 8 7 6 5 4 3 2 1

FIRST EDITION

Cover design by Tracy Patterson
Photographs of historic beads on pages 9–12 are courtesy of The Bead Museum, Washington, DC, Bead Timeline of History, photographed by Robert K. Liu
Frontispiece: Hollow eye bead by Louise Mehaffey

Library of Congress Cataloging-in-Publication Data

Mehaffey, Louise.
    Glass beads : tips, tools, and techniques for learning the craft / Louise Mehaffey ; photography by Kevin Brett.
        p cm.
    Includes bibliographical references.
    ISBN-13: 978-0-8117-0376-5 (hbk. : spiral bound)
    ISBN-10: 0-8117-0376-2 (hbk. : spiral bound)
  1. Glass craft. 2. Glass blowing and working. 3. Glass beads. I. Title.

TT298.M43 2008
748.8'5—dc22

                                              2007052939

CONTENTS

Projects 53

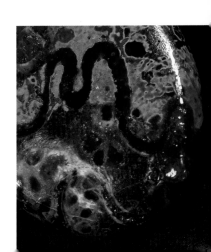

ACKNOWLEDGMENTS

All photographs in the chapter titled "A Brief History of Beads," except that of the dZi bead, are from the Bead Timeline of History at the Bead Museum in Washington, D.C., and were taken by Robert K. Liu of *Ornament* magazine. Special thanks to Hilary Whittaker for all her time and work involved in making the Bead Museum photographs available to me. The rest of the photographs in this book are by Kevin Brett, who caught some amazing action shots and learned more about lampworking than he ever thought he would know. Thanks, Kevin.

At Stackpole Books, thanks to editor Kyle Weaver, who created the Heritage Crafts Today series, for his work developing this volume with me, and his team of professionals, including copyeditor Joyce Bond, editorial assistant Brett Keener, designer Tracy Patterson, and art director Caroline Stover.

INTRODUCTION

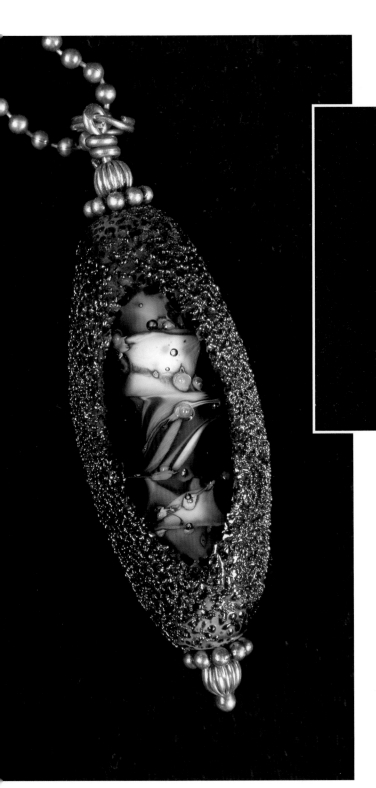

This book is about how I make my mandrel-wound, lampworked glass beads. "Mandrel-wound" means that I wrap the molten glass around a metal rod called a mandrel, which creates the hole in the bead. "Lampworking" refers to using a torch to melt the glass. Before the development of modern torches, oil and wax lamps were used; the worker typically blew through a metal tube to get the flame hot enough to melt the glass. This tradition is the origin of the term, although the technique is much older. Sometimes these beads are referred to as flameworked or torchworked.

There are other ways of making glass beads, such as fusing and casting, and glass also can be lampworked into sculptures, perfume bottles, and goblets, but the focus of this book is mandrel-wound, lampworked glass

Two elaborate beads by Louise Mehaffey.

Above: *Louise Mehaffey in her studio.*
Right: *The process of lampworking with a mandrel.*

beads. The beads can stand on their own as an art form or be used to create jewelry, either by simply stringing a few beads on a cord or making more elaborate pieces along with pearls, crystals, stone, or silver beads.

My obsession with glass started in the 1970s. My house had an ugly plastic sidelight beside the front door and I decided to replace it with a stained-glass panel, so I signed up for a workshop in stained glass and have been hooked on glass ever since. For more than twenty years, I operated a stained-glass studio, doing mostly residential commissions. During that time, I experimented with sandblasting glass, painting and firing it in a kiln, and fusing. A lampworking workshop in 1998 started me in that direction, and I now practice that craft exclusively.

Glass is a wonderfully versatile material for an artist. It can be worked cold by cutting, grinding, sand-blasting, painting, and engraving. It can be melted, shaped, and cast in a kiln. It can be worked in a furnace or with a torch and blown or shaped while molten. When it is cold, it is hard and brittle, but when it is molten, it is fluid.

The first several chapters talk about the use of glass beads historically and provide information on tools and equipment, basic skills, and bead shapes and colors. Most of the book is devoted to specific beads that you can make, starting with a simple round bead and pro-gressing to more difficult ones. I have tried to put the projects in order of difficulty, but many of the skills

overlap, and you can certainly work on them in any order you want. It's best to master a particular skill be-fore moving on. You may experience many hours or even days of frustration, but you will eventually catch on, so be persistent!

Over the years, I have developed my own unique style and way of working. This is not necessarily the right way and certainly not the only way. Like any other art worth learning, this is an art that takes practice, so don't be discouraged by wonky beads. Experiment. Learn to work with the glass, not fight it.

Warning: I am left-handed! Those of you who are right-handed will need to reverse hands from what's shown in the photos.

A Brief History of Beads

More than forty thousand years ago, early Stone Age humans strung some natural materials and created the first beads. These were probably found objects that had holes already in them or were easily pierced, such as seeds, shells, teeth, bones, and later coral and amber. People during this period also figured out how to pierce soft stones, and as advances in tools were made, they learned how to drill, polish, engrave, and carve harder stones.

Beads have served many purposes, and they can tell us much about the cultures that created and treasured them. One of their first uses was probably spiritual or ritualistic, and even today some bead designs are valued for the spiritual properties some believe they have. The color blue was considered particularly powerful by many cultures, and lapis lazuli stone beads were highly treasured. Faience beads were a distinctive blue color, and copper colored the early glass beads a beautiful shade of blue-green.

In some cultures, beads were invaluable for trade, as currency, and to record information. Certain colors or designs identified the wearers as members of a particular tribe or group or indicated wealth or status. There are many ancient styles or designs of beads that modern beadmakers use for inspiration.

Shells

Faience beads

FAIENCE BEADS

The ancient Egyptians became masters of a technique that involved compacting a powdered mineral, usually quartz, and covering it with a glass glaze to create faience beads, a forerunner of glass beads. The first glass beads were probably created around four thousand years ago, but their exact origin is unknown.

Melon beads

MELON BEADS

Melon beads are round or oval with longitudinal grooves carved from hole to hole. They were made from different stones, but those reserved for royalty were from lapis lazuli. In some ancient cultures, this stone indicated wealth and power, but it may have had other meanings in other cultures. Many burials dating

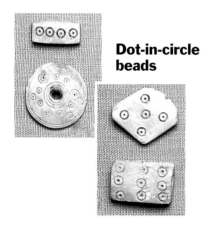

Dot-in-circle beads

Eye beads

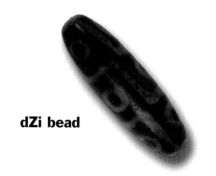

dZi bead

to 2450 BC at the Royal Cemetery of Ur in Mesopotamia had a single blue melon bead. This design is one that has lasted for thousands of years and is found in many cultures.

DOT-IN-CIRCLE BEADS

The dot-in-circle pattern is found on beads of many shapes and sizes, and among many cultures. It is so common that it seems likely to have had a powerful meaning, but the significance of this pattern is unknown. Some speculate that it was perhaps a forerunner to eye beads, but no research has been done to verify this.

EYE BEADS

Eye beads cross many cultures and centuries, surviving even today. The eye is commonly a symbol of protection from evil, but the symbology is complex and interpreted in different ways in different cultures. Common examples are from agate, with dark and light layers. These layered agate beads were copied by early glass beadmakers, who used successive layers of glass, with some beads having as many as twenty layers. There seems to have been a preference for a blue-green matrix with layers of blue and white or yellow topped by a dark blue spot. Eye beads with a yellow matrix and layers of white and blue topped by a dark blue spot were also common.

DZI BEAD

The very old dZi (pronounced "zee") beads are found mainly in Tibet and neighboring regions. They are made of etched black or brown agate, with a white line and eye pattern, and usually have a gently tapered barrel shape. These beads are revered and are believed to have a strong power to protect the wearer from evil. Tibetans have developed a rating system based on the style and quality of the bead, with the "pure" dZi at the top. Etched agate dZi beads below this are considered less important. Certain patterns are more prized than others. Tibetan owners seldom part with their dZi beads. Because of their value, there are many fake dZi beads on the market. The pictured dZi bead is a copy.

Warring state beads

WARRING STATE BEADS

Warring state beads were made by the Chinese around 480 to 220 BC, who then abruptly stopped making them. They are technically very elaborate and beautifully designed. The most common pattern is stratified eyes of various complexity connected by white dotted lines. The stratified eyes are often built up into protruding horns. This design possibly was influenced by eye beads, but its significance has been lost. Many copies of these beads can be found.

GOLD GLASS BEADS

Gold glass beads were an innovation of Hellenistic beadmakers, who covered clear colorless glass beads with gold foil. Early ones were a simple round shape; later the beads became segmented.

FACE BEADS

Early human face beads are commonly known as Phoenician and are found in the general Mediterranean area. There were probably production sites in several Phoenician cities. Styles varied greatly. Some had beards and others did not, leading to speculation that those without facial hair were female. Sometimes eyes were integral to the bead, but in other cases, they were applied slices of an eye cane.

MOSAIC BEADS

Mosaic, murrine, or cane beads cover a wide range of dates and cultures. The technique of combining different colors of glass into patterned blocks or canes was developed early in the history of glass beads. These canes were then cut into short segments or slices and applied to a hot glass bead. This technique is widely used today, and the slices are commonly called murrine or millefiori ("one thousand flowers"), reflecting the Italians' mastery of it. The first canes were probably a simple eye pattern, similar to a bull's-eye. Complex eye canes could be produced in large numbers, and less skilled beadmakers could then produce many beads with the same pattern.

Gold glass beads

Face beads

Mosaic beads

11

Mosaic face beads

Later, more complex canes were made, and a checkerboard pattern was often used. Whole faces were made into canes and then the slices were applied to beads.

Much information is available about the history of beads. If you are interested in learning more, the Bibliography and Resources sections list books and other avenues to explore.

Tools and Materials

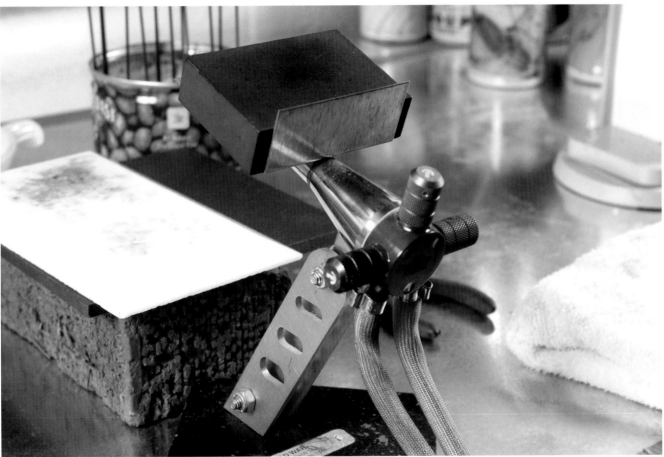

TORCH

Beadmaking torches are surface mix, which means the fuel gas and oxygen remain separate until they reach the torch tip. Probably the most widely used torch for beads is the Minor Bench Burner by Nortel. It is a very sturdy torch, and many beadmakers use it exclusively. Glass Torch Technology (GTT) makes the Bobcat and Lynx torches, Carlisle makes the Mini CC, and Bethlehem makes the Beadburner. These torches are ideal for soda-lime glass and can also work for borosilicate glass, but a larger torch, also available from these companies and others, is better if you're going to work with boro glass often or make larger pieces.

When I started, I tried using a Hot Head torch, which is made to be screwed onto the top of a Mapp gas cylinder. It is relatively inexpensive, and no other fuel is needed so it can be a good way to start out. The noise really bothered me, though, and it does not get very hot. A Hot Head torch melts the glass slowly, and I am very impatient, so after ten minutes, I turned it off and ordered a Minor. It can be ideal for a beginner, though, since it is slow and gives you time to work, and some beadmakers stay with it for years. I used my Minor for years and then moved to a GTT Lynx, which I love.

Don't agonize over which torch to buy. There is a very strong market for used torches, so if you decide you want a different one, you should be able to sell yours for not much less than you paid for it.

GLASS

Almost any kind of glass can be worked with a torch, but it isn't that simple. All glass expands as it is heated and contracts as it cools, and the rate at which it does so is called the coefficient of expansion (COE). This is usually expressed as a whole number, as in a COE of 104, and it measures how much a particular glass will expand at a certain temperature.

Two main types of glass are used by lampworkers: soda-lime and borosilicate. Soda-lime glass is a soft glass, which means it melts at a lower temperature, whereas borosilicate glass (Pyrex) is a hard glass, melting at a higher temperature. Generally, the higher the COE, the softer the glass.

Most glass used by lampworkers comes in the form of rods similar in diameter to a pencil, around 6 mm. Probably the majority of bead lampworkers use Effetre or Moretti glass. It is made in Italy and was known as Moretti for many years, but after the ownership changed several years ago, the name was changed, and

it is now called by either. It is a favorite glass because of the broad range of colors available and its workability in the flame. Spectrum and Bullseye are American companies that manufacture stained glass as well as lampworking glass. Northstar and Glass Alchemy manufacture borosilicate glass. New companies are now producing lines of glass compatible with those of established companies, so be on the lookout for new colors in compatible glass. Just remember that not all the glass from one company is necessarily compatible. Be sure to use glass that has the same COE, or enough stress can be created to crack the glass. If you use different COE glass in your studio, keep them clearly marked and store them separately. Having said all this, because the mass of beads is relatively small and because of their shape, glass with COEs within several points can usually be used together with no problem.

Some common lampworking glass and their COEs are Effetre or Moretti, 104; Spectrum, 96; Bullseye, 90; Northstar, 32–33; and Glass Alchemy, 32–33.

Glass is made in batches, and each batch can vary in color. Some colors are very predictable, but others can vary considerably every time you order them.

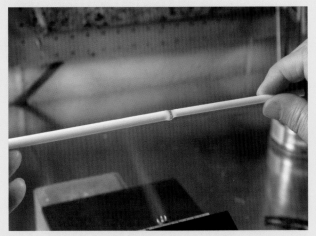

In general, the opaque colors are softer, which means they melt at a lower temperature, and the transparent colors are harder. At the top of the soft glass list is white. White stringers—thin, spaghetti-like rods of glass—are very difficult to control, and some techniques can be hard to accomplish on a white base bead because its surface can get too soft. White is often used under transparent colors to highlight them. When it is hot, it becomes clear (above).

Opaque red glass becomes black when it is heated (above), so it's very difficult to make a red and black bead.

Transparent cobalt blue is stiffer than most colors, which means it melts at a higher temperature. Therefore, dots or stringers of this color can be easier to control.

Black is really a transparent color, a very dark violet. If it becomes thin, it will no longer be black. Intense black was developed to overcome this problem. This glass will remain black even if stretched thin, but it is expensive, so it is usually sold in stringers. It becomes fuzzy if it gets too hot.

Ivory glass comes in light and dark. Light ivory is a beautiful cream color and quite stable. Dark ivory is very reactive, which means it has a chemical reaction with some colors and metals, especially silver foil or leaf. One of the projects in this book is making a silver stringer with dark ivory glass, and then using that stringer on a bead. Even by itself, a dark ivory bead will have color variations.

Sometimes a reaction will occur between colors. If you use colors with copper in them (most of the blues and greens) with sulfur colors (most of the ivories, reds, oranges, and yellows), there will be a dark line wherever they touch. A bead of ivory with a melted dot of sky blue will have a dark line around the blue dot. If you don't want this effect, you can simply put a clear or light transparent dot on the ivory first so that the blue dot doesn't touch the ivory.

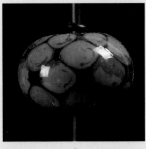

If glass with copper in it is overheated or worked in a flame with too much propane, it will develop red streaks. Turquoise and sky blue are particularly susceptible to this. Sometimes you can get the copper streaks to disappear by gently reheating the glass.

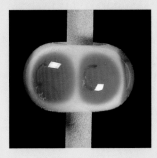

Some colors bleed and won't make crisp lines. Greens in particular tend to bleed, and white can also be problematic, especially if it is heated too much.

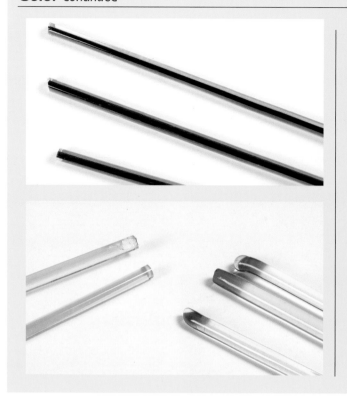

Filigrana is a rod of clear glass with a line of color in the center (top). Using a stringer of black filigrana for making a design on a bead results in a very thin black line, since our eyes don't read the clear glass. Filigranas are also used in making fancy canes, thinner rods of glass twisted or assembled into patterns.

Some glass comes in striking colors, which change when the glass in heated, or struck (bottom). If you buy striking red rods, for instance, they will look like a light transparent amber glass. When you use this glass, you first make your bead and strike the color by allowing it to cool a little, then reheating it. It will become a beautiful transparent red. I always strike the ends of this glass when I buy it so I don't mix it up with nonstriking colors.

Layering glass colors can result in new colors. It is not the same as mixing paint colors, and sometimes the results are surprising, so experiment!

PROPANE

Most beadmakers use a barbecue propane tank, but you can use natural gas if it is available. For safety reasons, this tank should never be stored inside.

OXYGEN

For oxygen, contact a local gas supply company. Buying the oxygen in larger tanks is much more cost effective than the smaller ones, but they can be hard to handle. Some companies require you to purchase a tank, others will lease it, and most will deliver, though some will not deliver to a residential address. Oxygen is not a flammable gas; it is an accelerant, which makes the flame burn hotter. Do not use any oil or oil product around the oxygen, as it can spontaneously ignite. Oxygen tanks must be chained in place when in use, because if the valve stem on the top of the tank were damaged, it could become a missile, so carefully consider where you will set it up. The cap should be on when the tank is not in use and any time the tank is being moved.

OXYGEN CONCENTRATOR

Beadmakers now have the option of using oxygen concentrators or generators in place of the oxygen tanks, and they generally work well for the torches. Most of them are about the size of a dehumidifier and run on household current. The concentrators are generally from the medical industry and refurbished, although some companies now offer new concentrators and generators appropriate for lampworking. These suppliers have been changing on a regular basis, so check the website of the International Society of Glass Bead Makers and the companies in the Supplies section in the back of this book for current sources.

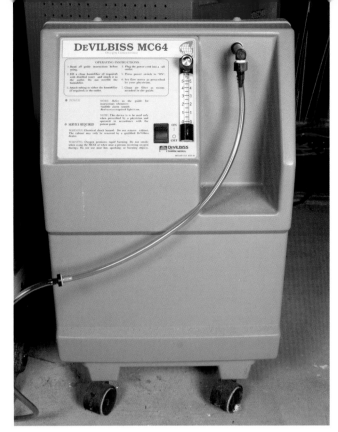

HOSES

To connect your torch to a gas and oxygen supply, you need two rubber hoses, which you can purchase from a gas supply company. If you're using propane, get type T. Another common type is rated for acetylene, but propane gas will cause that rubber to deteriorate, so do not use it. Usually $1/4$-inch ID (inner diameter) is needed with B fittings, depending on your torch. The two hoses come in a package of 10 or 25 feet and are connected together, a red one for flammable gas and a green one for oxygen. One end usually has a brass B-style fitting that will screw onto the regulator, and the other end is cut. The cut end is pressed onto the torch fitting and attached with a hose clamp.

REGULATORS

To control the pressure coming from your tanks, you need two regulators–one for the propane tank and one for the oxygen tank. Usually the propane regulator has only one valve, which measures the pressure in the hose going to the torch, although mine has two. One 20-pound propane tank will last quite a while. The oxygen regulator has two valves, one that measures the tank pressure and another that regulates the pressure going to the torch. A new oxygen tank will have around 2,200 pounds per square inch (psi) of pressure. Generally the propane is set between 4 and 8 psi and the oxygen between 8 and 16 psi. What pressures to use depends on your preference and your torch, so check its directions.

In order to make the projects in this book, you need to use a lampworking studio. You can set up your own, following the guidelines below, or find a local studio where you can work.

The torches used for lampworking require a fuel gas—usually propane—and oxygen. *Warning*: For safety reasons, the required tanks must be kept outside, with the hoses or pipes run into the studio. Safety precautions are very important for all lampworkers. Check for leaks at all the connections after your system is hooked up and every time you change tanks or make any other changes. Propane leaks can be especially dangerous, since propane is heavier than air and will collect at the lowest part of your studio. For ventilation, most beadmakers use a hood similar to a stove hood or bathroom fan. If you notice an odor, feel dizzy, or develop a headache when you have been working, your ventilation is not good enough.

Your torch should always be attached to a sturdy table so you can't accidentally knock it over. I use a C clamp so I can easily remove it. The table or workbench and the floor should be nonflammable, and also check the area for anything flammable and remove it. Place a working fire extinguisher where you can get to it in case of a fire. Wear natural fiber clothing, tie long hair back, and don't work with long fingernails. Have some aloe or burn cream available for minor burns.

Some other considerations can make your workbench more comfortable for lampworking. Adequate light will prevent eyestrain. I have a fluorescent light overhead, a swing-arm lamp on one side, and a full-spectrum light on the other. Your workbench and chair should be at a good height for you. Having an office chair that is adjustable makes that easier. Don't bend your wrists when working, or you may develop carpal tunnel syndrome. Experiment with positions to find one that doesn't stress your shoulders.

Various armrests are on the market; I use a folded towel under one elbow, which helps with my shoulder position and also prevents blisters on my elbow. The angle of the torch can also be adjusted to a comfortable position for you.

Behind my torch, I have a 6 x 6-inch graphite square, called a marver, that I put on a brick to raise it up. I roll hot glass on this marver to shape it and use it as a heat sink to cool hot glass. It's also a handy place to lay metal foil or leaf I will be using on a bead. A small graphite marver is also mounted on my torch. Behind the bench marver, I put a small Pyrex glass bowl of water for cooling off hot tools or fingers. I also drop bits of hot glass into it to keep them off my workbench. For larger pieces of hot glass, I have a metal can on the floor. To one side of the torch, I have a tool rest for the glass I am using and several coffee mugs for my tools to help keep them organized.

Within reach are also various containers with a selection of glass rods. Most of my rods are stored on the other side of my studio. I created storage bins by cutting rectangular plastic downspouts into 14-inch lengths and stacking them in a sturdy wood cube. Other plastic pipes can also work well for this purpose. This system lets me see at a glance which colors I need to order.

Each situation is different and requires different solutions. The best way to set up a studio is to consult an expert to help you make the connections and use your system correctly. Your gas or lampworking supplier is usually willing to help and can be a great source for information. But be sure to educate yourself, because you are the one who will be responsible for it. Check online at the websites of the International Society of Beadmakers (www.isgb.org) and the lampworking suppliers in the Supplies and Resources section. Get some books and read them. A wealth of information is available, so take the time to learn to be safe.

KILNS

Many kilns are on the market for beadmakers, and it can be difficult to choose one. The best allow you to place the beads in the kiln while they are still on the mandrel. Two important things are that it runs on household current, or you may have to do some house rewiring, and that the elements are encased so you can't accidentally touch them with a metal mandrel. Most kilns now come with a digital controller, which makes annealing easier, but I used my kiln for years without one. My favorite model is the Toolbox Kiln from Don McKinney of the Glass Palette, although he no longer makes them. Similar kilns, however, are on the market. I also have a firebrick kiln that I use as a backup for beads, as well as for fusing and casting. Choose carefully, and your kiln will give you many years of service.

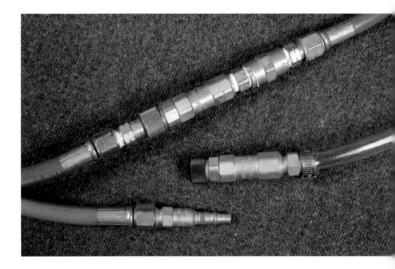

QUICK CONNECTS

Quick connects make connecting and disconnecting torches, regulators, and hoses fast and easy, and they have reverse flow check valves built in. I use them to disconnect my torch from my system when I want to travel with it.

FLASHBACK ARRESTORS

Use flashback arrestors in the hose lines. They have a check valve built in to stop reverse flow and prevent mixing of fuel gas and oxygen, and they also prevent any flame from reaching the tanks. The arrestors usually come in pairs, one for the propane line and one for the oxygen line. Typically they are installed between the hose and the regulator.

MANDRELS

Mandrels are stainless steel welding rods. Three sizes are commonly used by beadmakers: $1/8$, $3/32$, and $1/16$ inch. You can buy them already cut to a working length (9 to 12 inches) from any lamp-working supplier or buy welding rods from your gas supplier and cut them yourself. If you cut them yourself, you need to file the burrs off the cut ends. I find 9-inch rods too short and prefer 12-inch. Thinner rods will bend much more easily than thicker ones. If a rod bends, you should discard it, because you can't make a well-balanced bead on a bent mandrel. Sometimes bead release won't stick to new mandrels; if so, just clean the surface or roughen it up with very fine steel wool.

GLASSES

Always wear eye protection, since glass can fly in unexpected directions.

When the glass is in the flame, it produces a bright orange light called sodium flare, and didymium glasses will both protect your eyes and reduce the sodium flare so you can see the glass. There are now other kinds of glasses in addition to didymium, and all can be made with prescription lenses. Any of the lampworking suppliers can help you choose the correct glasses for the type of work you will be doing. Because my eyeglass prescription changes frequently, I opted to work with a shield that sits just above my torch. I look through the shield when melting glass and can wear my prescription safety eyeglasses. As an added bonus, the shield blocks some of the heat from the torch.

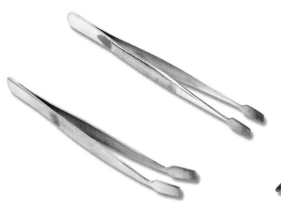

TWEEZERS

I have three or four sizes of tweezers for torch work. Tweezers can be ridged or smooth inside the tips, and both can be useful.

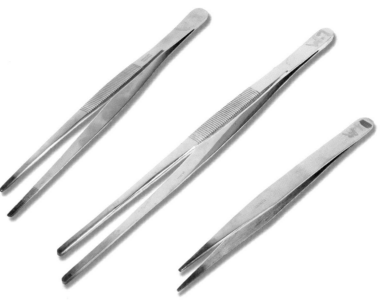

PLIERS

One of my favorite tools is a cheap pair of jewelry pliers. I use the pliers to pull stringers (a spaghetti-like rod of glass), and they are thick enough to thermal shock hot glass, useful at times.

BEAD RELEASE

If hot glass touches the metal mandrel, it will fuse to it. Bead release is a thick liquid clay mixture that will withstand the high temperatures of the torch and allow the bead to be removed from the mandrel. You'll find many brands on the market both for general use and for specific situations. Some can be flame-dried and others must be air-dried. There are formulations to hold the bead tightly, which will help prevent the bead release from breaking while you are working on it, and others that will release the bead easily. I have found Bead Fusion to be good for general use, and it can be flame-dried. That means I can dip mandrels, dry them in the flame, and start working right away.

21

MARVERS AND PADDLES

Hot glass doesn't stick to graphite, so it is used to marver, or shape, the glass. You need a graphite marver on your bench, around 6 x 6 inches, laid on something nonflammable like a brick to raise it up to a useful height. I also have a small marver mounted on my torch. Graphite paddles come in various shapes and sizes. My favorite one is long enough to roll the bead on, but not so long as to be too heavy. Brass paddles grip the glass better than graphite, so they work really well for moving hot glass. All of these can be used as a heat sink. If the glass is too hot, touch it with the graphite or brass to absorb some of the heat.

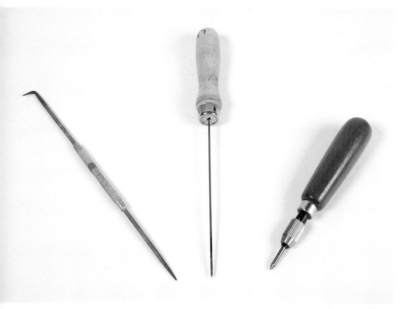

PICKS, POKES, AND RAKES

Picks, pokes, and rakes of various thicknesses are useful as well, or you can sharpen the end of a mandrel. These tools are used to touch hot glass and pull it into a pattern or poke a design in the glass. Dental tools can be used, but they are so thin that they melt easily.

STRIKERS AND MATCHES

I usually use a striker to light my torch, but sometimes I use matches. Beginners usually find matches a little easier to use, but once you get the knack of the striker, it is clean and inexpensive. There are other lighters on the market too, so look around. I don't like butane lighters, though, as the body of the lighter could melt if some hot glass fell on it.

BENCH BRUSH

You will need a bench brush to clean your bench surface. I use a soft paintbrush and sweep the chips into a metal can on the floor. I also have a smaller brush that is useful for cleanup of powdered enamels and frits (crushed glass).

SQUASHERS

Squashers are used to flatten hot glass. They come in various sizes. You will probably need both a small and a large one. You can also use a lentil squasher to create lentil-shaped beads. New small squashers have two square plates. A friend melted the brass plate off one side of my small squasher (don't put your tools in the flame!) and silver soldered a round plate back on for me. Some large ones have a set screw to set a squashing depth, but I have never used it. My favorite squasher is actually a pair of ice tongs, but unfortunately, I haven't been able to find them for sale anymore.

ROD CUTTERS

Rod cutters are handy for cutting rods of glass to a working length. Some suppliers ship glass rods already cut to 13 or 14 inches, but others ship them at their full length of 1 meter (39.37 inches) and you will need to cut them yourself. Tile nippers can also be used to cut rods.

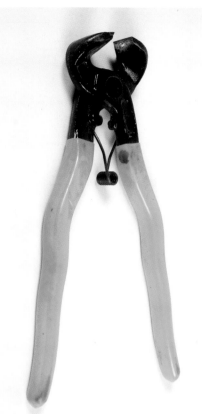

ROD RESTS

Rod rests are made of stainless steel. I have two on my bench to lay glass rods on and one in my kiln for the end of the mandrel when placing a bead in the kiln.

PARING KNIFE AND
OTHER MISCELLANEOUS TOOLS

Tools for working with hot glass can be found in unusual places. One of my favorite tools is a small paring knife I bought at the grocery store. It is just the right size and shape for creasing hot glass. Textured surfaces can be great to roll hot glass on. Just be sure anything that comes in contact with hot glass is made from graphite, stainless steel, brass, or copper. Don't use galvanized metals or zinc, which can put off toxic fumes.

SPOONS, METAL ASHTRAYS,
AND SAUCERS

Spoons are useful for holding frits and enamels while rolling a bead. To hold frits, I bend little metal ashtrays into more of a cup shape, and then put them on china saucers or small plates to keep the frits from spilling on the workbench.

Basic Skills

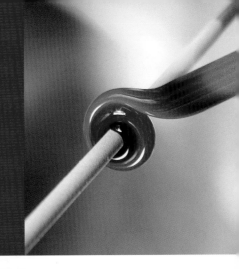

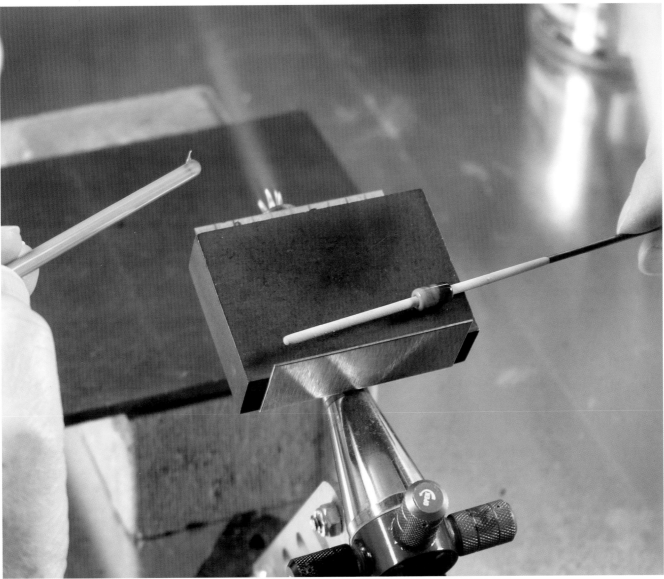

Once your studio is set up, you have your glass and supplies, and your torch is ready to go, you need to learn the basic skills involved in making glass beads: dipping mandrels, cleaning your glass, lighting and using the torch, shaping the bead, annealing, and flame annealing.

One of the first things to do when getting ready to work is to dip some mandrels in the bead release. The release should have the consistency of yogurt or a little thinner and be smooth. If it gets too thick, add some clean water and shake. If it is too thin, leave the lid off so it can dry out somewhat. I like to use a tall, thin olive jar for dipping mandrels, because it does not expose much surface to the air, which helps keep the release from drying out. Shake the jar well, and dip the mandrel straight down and up. Doing this fast will create a thicker coating, and slower dips will result in a thinner coat. Be particular, because if the coating is bumpy, the bead hole will be bumpy, and if a spot flakes off, the glass will fuse to the metal.

After dipping, place each mandrel in a can of sand to hold it upright and not touching anything. Some beadmakers use a piece of wood with holes drilled in it. I try to dip enough mandrels to last through a torch session. How many you need depends on what kinds of beads you plan to make. Small, simple beads can be made much faster than large, complex ones. Six is a good number to start. You can always dip more. If you dip too many, try to use them within a few days. I don't really know how long a dipped mandrel can sit, but I don't want to take a chance on the release failing.

The bead release must be air-dried or flame-dried before adding glass. If the release you are using doesn't say it can be flame-dried, don't do it. The release I use can be flame-dried, but I still like to let it air-dry a little. To flame-dry it, wave it in and out of the flame to dry it gradually. If you heat it up too fast, it can flake off, exposing bare metal. You can easily see the color of the release change as it dries.

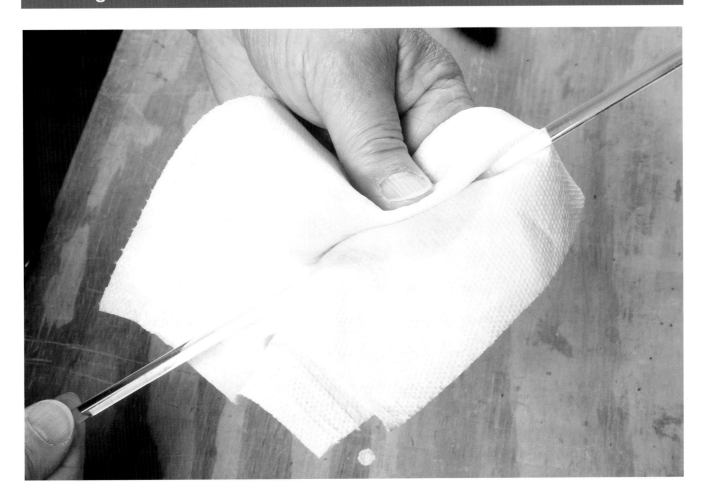

After you choose the glass rods you will be using to make your beads, clean them if needed. If the rods are dirty, that dirt will become part of your bead. You can use a paper towel or cloth with rubbing alcohol or glass cleaner on it. Keep rubbing alcohol off your workbench, though, since it is flammable. Don't use rubber bands to bundle your glass rods—they can deteriorate and leave residue on the glass that is hard to remove. Inexpensive ponytail holders are great for bundling glass rods. Having clean glass is especially important with clear and light transparent colors, since any dirt will be even more obvious.

Before lighting the torch, first turn on your ventilation. If you are using matches, light the match before turning the propane valve to avoid having propane come into your workspace. To light the torch, think of the acronym POOP, for propane/oxygen/oxygen/propane. The first two letters are the correct order to light the torch, and the last two letters are the order to turn it off.

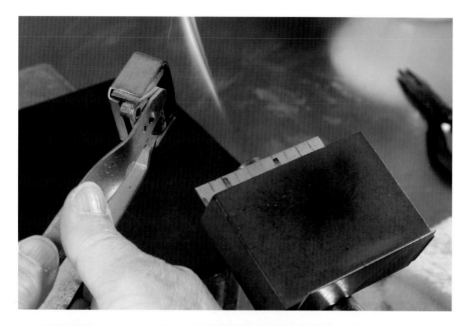

In other words, light the propane first and adjust the flame to about a hand length, 6 to 7 inches long. Then gently turn on the oxygen valve. When you are ready to turn your flame off, first turn off the oxygen and then the propane. Turn the valves slowly so that you will recognize if you are turning them the wrong way. Turn them gently and don't crank them shut. Some torches have more than two valves; refer to the directions for that torch. Usually the propane valves are red or orange, and the oxygen valves are green.

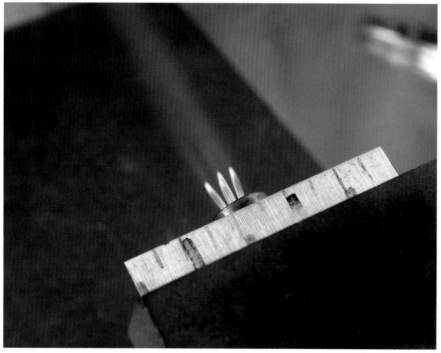

Setting the correct flame is important. It is a little different for each torch, so take the time to learn about the one you are using. If the flame has too much of either propane or oxygen, it can affect the glass. Look at your flame and you will see little "rods" coming from the torch, around $1/4$ to $1/2$ inch long. These are called the cones. The cones should be sharp, with just a little yellow on their tips. If they are fuzzy and have a lot of yellow, there is too much propane. Either turn down the propane or turn up the oxygen. If there is no yellow at all and you hear a loud hiss, the oxygen is too high. Turn down the oxygen or turn up the propane.

Most of the time, you should work in a neutral flame, with the two gases in balance. If more propane is added, it becomes a reduction flame and is not as hot, which can cause some glass to become sooty. If too much oxygen is added, it becomes an oxidizing flame, which is also a cooler flame and is used for some special techniques. Learn to set your flame correctly and to adjust it larger or smaller, depending on what you are doing.

You should generally work with your glass 2 to 3 inches from the torch tip. Don't work too close. If you get some glass on the tip, turn the torch off immediately, let it cool, and carefully chip the glass away, being sure none of the ports are clogged. If you can't get all the ports cleared, contact your supplier for help.

Two forces to understand when working with molten glass to shape your bead are surface tension and gravity. Surface tension pulls the glass into a rounded shape, and gravity pulls it down. The mandrel must be constantly turned to fight gravity and keep a balanced bead; the hotter the glass, the faster you need to turn the mandrel.

A well-shaped bead has smooth, puckered holes with no sharp edges. The key to accomplishing this shape is in the footprint, the area of contact where the glass touches the mandrel.

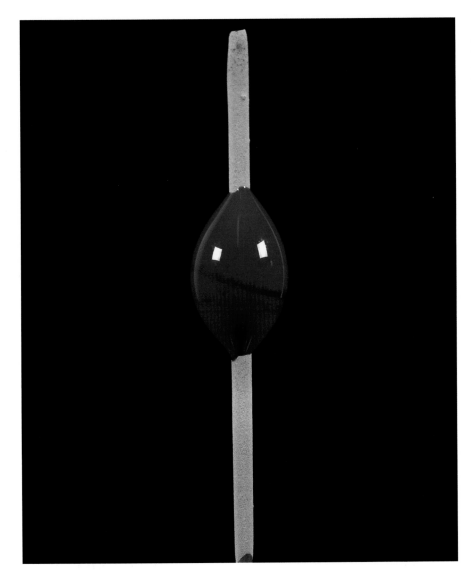

If the footprint is too wide for the amount of glass in the bead, when the glass is heated, the surface tension pulls it up into a rounded shape and leaves the ends thin and ragged. Glass flows toward the heat, so if you make a long bead and then concentrate the flame on the center of the bead, the glass will flow toward the center, creating an olive shape with thin ends. To fix this problem, either add more glass or start over with a narrower footprint.

When the glass rod you are using gets too short to use, you can join it to a new one and continue to use it. Heat the ends of both the short and new pieces to get them molten.

Then touch them together.

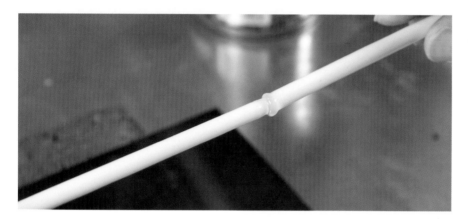

Pull them slightly apart.

Hold straight until the glass is rigid. If you hold the joined rods vertically, they will line up naturally. The joint will be more prone to cracking, so don't use this part of the rod when you are doing something delicate.

Some Safety Tips

- For safety, always place glass rods and tools with the hot ends away from you so that you won't accidentally pick up a hot end. I lay the glass rods I am using on a tool rest so that dirt or stray glass chips won't adhere to them if the ends are still soft.
- Never put your tools in the flame. Almost all work is done out of the flame, not in it. Most beginners work the glass much too hot. If a metal tool becomes too hot, the glass will stick to it, so occasionally dip the ends of the tool into the water dish to cool them.
- Keep the ends of your glass rods neat. When I am done working with a rod, I roll it on a marver to shape it. I am not too picky about it, but if the rod has a large glob of glass on its end, it will be much more difficult to introduce it into the flame without an explosion (see the photo below).

- Never, ever reach in front of your torch, even when it is off. Most torches are very quiet, and sometimes the flame is hard to see. Eventually you may think it is off and put your hand in the flame.
- Treat burns quickly. You will get burned, so be prepared. Immediately put a burn into cold water, such as the water dish on your workbench. If it's a minor burn, you can apply aloe or some other burn cream, wrap it with a bandage, and continue working. Even small burns are very sensitive to heat, and the bandage will help keep the heat of the flame from the burn. If it is a serious burn, consult a physician immediately. Burns can become infected easily and can take a long time to heal.
- Pay attention to where you are working in the flame. By looking for the sodium flare, you should be able to see where the flame is hitting the glass.

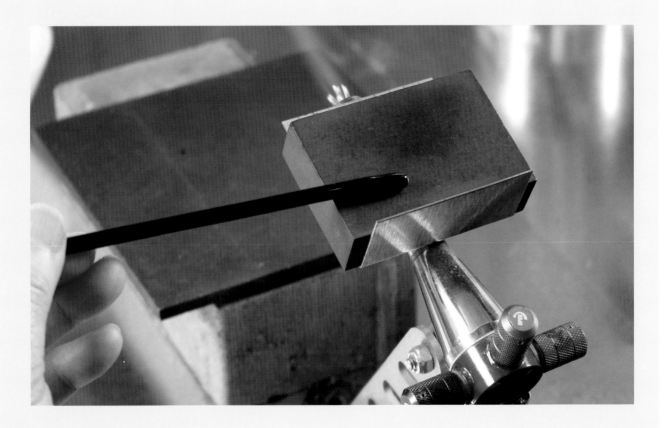

For your first bead, start with the simplest shape—the basic round bead. Lampworking is like patting your head and rubbing your stomach at the same time! You need to work with both hands and be aware of what each one is doing. Remember to work several inches from the torch head.

Begin by choosing a glass rod and holding it in your dominant hand like a pencil, about 3 or 4 inches from the working end. If you hold the rod farther up, it is hard to control. Both glass and stainless steel mandrels are poor conductors of heat, so you can hold them rather close to the working end.

Hold the mandrel in your other hand in an overhand position. Curl the last fingers of your hand to rest the mandrel on, and use your thumb and index finger to roll the mandrel away from you. Practice this before putting it in the flame. Heat the mandrel in the flame where the glass will be added, an inch or so from the end. If the metal is not hot, the glass won't stick. Keep the mandrel warm, either below or at the edge of the flame.

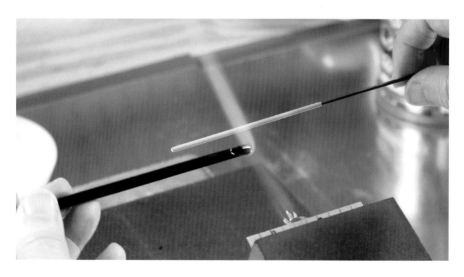

Slowly introduce the tip of the glass rod to the flame. If you heat it too fast, it will thermal shock and spit glass. You can quickly wave the end in and out of the flame or use the cooler upper part of the flame. Get the end of the glass rod molten, but don't get a large gather, or glob of glass, or the footprint will be too wide. Try to keep the diameter of the gather the same as that of the rod, and heat the rod until the tip starts to droop.

Some Tips

- It can be hard to see the bottom of the flame, so watch for the red glow of the mandrel or bead. By working with the glass rod on the side of the flame, it is easy to move in and out to adjust its temperature.
- If the bead becomes too molten, lower it a little. If it gets too hot, it will be very hard to control, and the glass can actually boil. If the mandrel or glass turns really bright orange or white, it is too hot.
- Some colors thermal shock more easily when introduced to the flame. If you are having trouble with a particular rod, try preheating its tip in your kiln.

- Keep turning the mandrel, even when you think the bead is rigid.
- Think of the heat from the flame as a tool, and learn to use it.
- Don't let your bead get too cool while working, or it will thermal shock when you put it back in the flame. If you think it may have become too cool, put it back in the flame slowly and at the outer, cooler edge of the flame. Eventually you will develop an internal timer that lets you know how long you can keep the bead out of the flame before it needs to be heated again.

Position the mandrel just underneath the flame and hold it horizontal. Don't work with the mandrel directly in the flame. If you do, you will burn right through it. Point the glass rod at the mandrel and through the flame or on the side of it. Heating the rod through the flame can feed hot glass continually onto the mandrel.

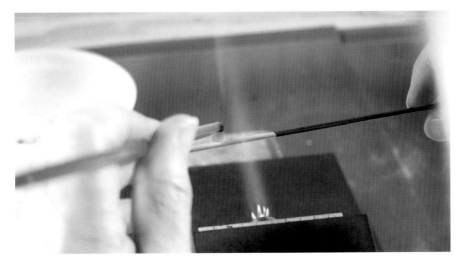

Lightly touch the molten glass to the mandrel.

Roll the mandrel away from you until you have a complete wrap or run out of hot glass.

Don't pull on the glass when it hardens, or the bead release may break. If it does break, immediately stop working, as the hot bead can slide down the rod onto your hand.

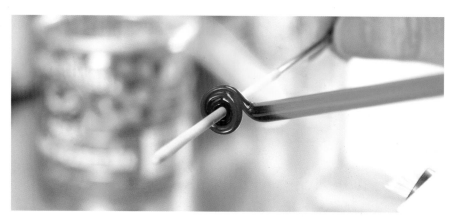

Flame-cut the rod by aiming the flame where you want it to separate. I usually pull the rod a little while the glass is still molten so that it thins and will separate quickly in the flame.

If you want a larger bead, heat up more glass and add it by touching it to the bead and rolling the mandrel away from you. At this point, it doesn't matter if you add the glass on the side or top of the bead, since it will all melt into a round bead, but try to add the glass evenly around the bead. Don't touch the glass rod to the mandrel unless you want to make your footprint wider.

When you are done adding glass, turn the bead to evenly heat it and get it round. Keep the bead in the top or bottom of the flame—it doesn't need to be entirely in it. As you are turning the bead, pause slightly when the larger side is up.

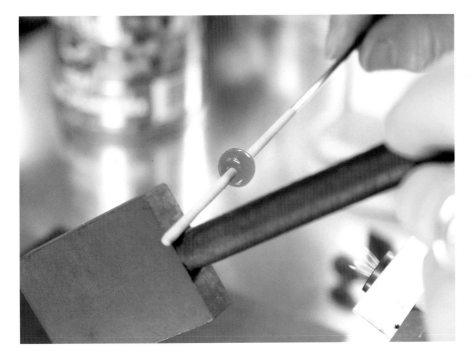

Putting the end of the mandrel in the L of the graphite paddle and handle can help you balance the glass and see what side is larger. I make my beads about an inch from the end of the mandrel so there is room to do this. If you are using opaque glass, watch the horizon of the bead as you are turning to see if it is balanced. If your glass is transparent, watch the distance between the mandrel and the edge of the bead as you are turning. Don't let the glass get too hot, or you will lose control. Heat the bead and then take it out of the flame while you are turning. You don't need to work in the flame all the time.

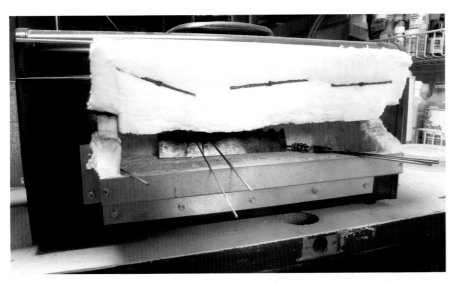

When you are finished shaping your bead, wait for the glass to get rigid before putting it in the kiln, but keep turning it. With Moretti glass, the bead is getting rigid when the glow has just faded. I like to put the end of the mandrel on a tool rest in the kiln so that the glass won't get marred if it is still a little soft. By the time I finish the next bead, it will be rigid and can be moved to one side of the kiln. Make as many beads as you want, following this same process.

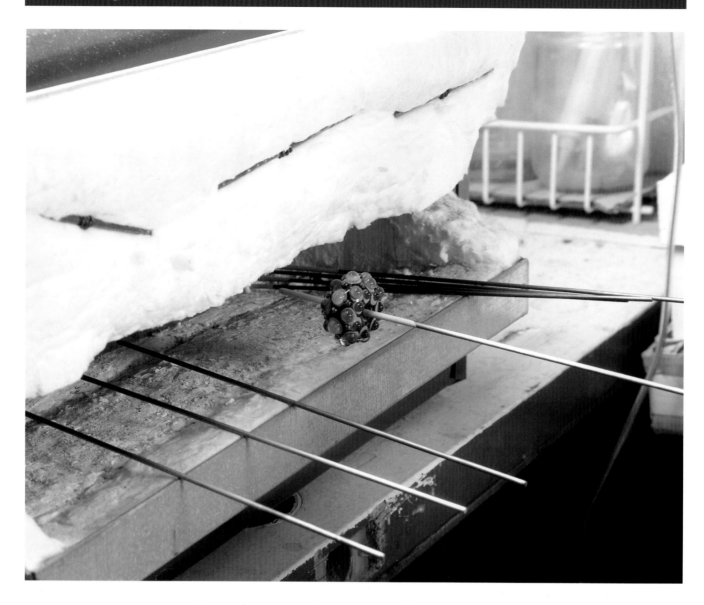

Simply stated, annealing is the controlled, even cooling of glass. Because beads have a relatively small mass and because of their shape, the annealing schedule is not as rigorous as it is for larger glass pieces. But if the beads are not annealed, enough stress can remain to cause cracks. This can occur immediately or weeks or even months later!

Glass has three temperature points that are important: the strain, annealing, and softening points. These temperature points are in actuality a range and are not absolute. As the glass is heated from room temperature, it reaches the strain point first. Here the molecules begin to move around, but the glass is still rigid. As the glass becomes hotter, it moves through the annealing range to the softening point, when it becomes soft. At a working temperature, the molecules in the glass are moving freely. Bringing the temperature back down, as the bead cools, the softening point is reached first. Below this temperature, the glass is now rigid, but the molecules are still moving. The outside of the bead cools and hardens faster than the inside, where the molecules are still moving, and this difference creates stress. As the temperature drops more, the annealing point is reached next. This is the temperature at which all the molecules settle into their patterns relatively quickly. Continuing down, the strain point is reached. Once below this temperature, no more significant molecular movement occurs, so no more stress can be relieved. Thermal shock can occur if the temperature of the beads drops too fast, however, just like dropping ice cubes into a warm glass of water.

Annealing schedules can vary widely, and beadmakers all have their personal favorite. The ideal method is to place the bead in a kiln held at the annealing temperature immediately after finishing it and maintain this temperature long enough to ensure that the entire bead is the same temperature. Generally this is fifteen minutes for every $1/4$ inch of glass thickness, and thirty minutes is long enough for most beads. Then the kiln is slowly cooled to the strain point and typically held there for fifteen minutes or so. At this point, most kilns can be turned off, and the beads will cool to room temperature slowly enough not to cause thermal shock. In practice, beads can't be overannealed, so don't worry about using a longer schedule.

The larger the mass of glass, the slower the schedule needs to be. It also needs to be slower if the bead has protruding parts, like the fins of fish, because the small, thin parts will lose heat much faster than the body of the bead.

If no kiln is available when the beads are made, you can do batch annealing. As the beads are made, wait until they are rigid, and then put them into vermiculite or between layers of fiber blanket. This will slow down their cooling. Later they can be put into a cold kiln, slowly raised to the annealing point, and put through an annealing schedule. Using vermiculite or fiber blanket is not a substitute for annealing, however.

Here is an annealing schedule I use for Moretti glass. I set the kiln at 950 degrees, the approximate annealing temperature, and as each bead is finished, I put it into the kiln. When finished for the day, I hold the temperature there for thirty minutes, and then slowly reduce the temperature so that it takes about one and a half hours to reach 850, the strain point. I hold it there for fifteen minutes to equalize the glass temperature, and then turn off the kiln. When it is at room temperature, I can take my beads out and admire them. This is an aggressive schedule, but it has worked well for me.

FLAME ANNEALING

Flame annealing is a different process that also has to do with controlling the temperature of the glass. When you are finished making a bead, it is not an even temperature. It is hotter where you were just working and cooler where you were not. To even out the temperature before putting the bead in the kiln, turn it in the outer, cooler part of the flame of your torch until the temperature is equalized. Turn it quickly so that the bead doesn't get hot enough to melt and change your design. Then put it in the kiln to be annealed. Beads that especially need to be flame annealed are those with protruding parts, such as fish-shaped or long beads.

There are several mistakes beginners often make. Use the proper technique to avoid these pitfalls. You also need to know how to solve some common problems you're likely to encounter.

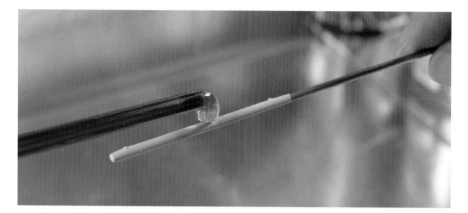

When adding glass, don't hold the glass rod parallel to the mandrel; the rod should be pointing at it.

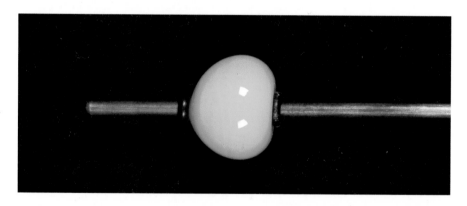

Don't slant the mandrel, which will result in a pear-shaped bead.

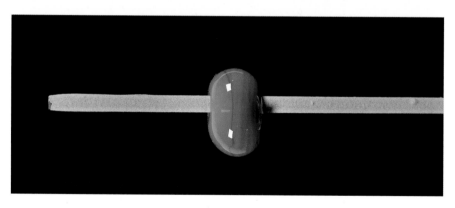

Turning unevenly or not turning long enough will create an unbalanced bead. Keep turning, even when you think the glass is rigid. Getting the bead too hot can result in losing control. If there isn't enough glass for the width of the footprint, you will wind up with an olive-shaped bead.

Cracks can occur when part of the bead gets too cool or when a cool part of the bead is put back into the flame too fast. Usually you will hear a little ping, and sometimes you will even feel the glass crack. Try heating the crack to heal it. This will distort any design on the bead, however. The closer the crack is to the surface of the bead, the easier it will be to heal it.

Air bubbles will occur. Small ones can just be part of the process, but large ones are distracting and can make your bead unstable. You can avoid most air bubbles by having the rod molten when adding glass to your bead. Bubbles near the surface can be heated and pinched out with tweezers. If they are too deep for that, try getting the glass really hot. Sometimes the bubble will be absorbed and disappear. Ultimately you need to decide how big is too big and how many is too many.

Scum, or lots of tiny bubbles in the glass, can occur if you overheat the glass. You have actually boiled it.

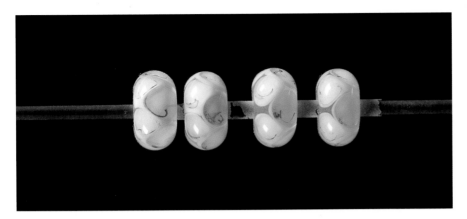

If you see what looks like dirt or soot in the glass, you probably had too much propane in your flame. Some colors are very sensitive to this, especially the transparent blues.

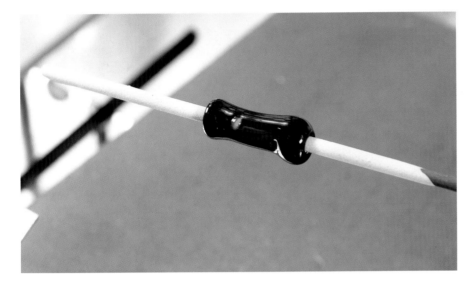

Sometimes the bead release flakes and gets in the glass while it is molten.

If you aren't too far along in the design and the release is on the surface, you can heat up that spot and pluck out the release with tweezers.

When you are finished making beads for the day, start the annealing program on your kiln. With my kiln and the annealing program I use, it is at least five hours before my beads are cool enough to take out of the kiln, so it is often the next morning before I see them.

So that you can start work with a clean bench next time, put the glass rods and tools back in their proper places, then use a bench brush to clean all the glass chips from the bench and the marvers. Close the tanks, burn off the propane in the hose, and release any oxygen from the other hose.

After the kiln has cooled down to room temperature, remove your beads and admire them. It's hard to be patient, but don't take them out until they are cool enough to be comfortably held. Put the mandrels with the beads in water to wet the bead release and keep the dust down, as breathing clay dust can be hazardous. Don't put warm beads in cold water. If they are still warm, then the water should be warm.

One by one, hold each mandrel with pliers and use your other hand to twist the bead loose. Scrub the bead up and down the mandrel and rinse it off. This cleans the bead release out of the hole in the bead and also helps keep the mandrel smooth. Some beadmakers also use a drill to further clean the bead hole.

If the bead won't come loose, wrap it with cloth to get a better grip or try letting it soak. Once I had to soak a bead for a month before I finally got it off. You might try putting it in the freezer, on the theory that the metal mandrel will contract faster than the glass. For really stubborn beads, I use a cordless drill. I put the mandrel in the drill, tighten the chuck, wrap the bead with a thick cloth to hold it, and start the drill. But be extremely careful doing this, or you can take a chunk out of your fingers.

If the bead won't come loose no matter what you try, you now have a nice plant pick! There can be several reasons why this happened. The bead release may have been too thick or thin and cracked or chipped, allowing the glass to touch the metal. Or you might have overheated the glass and mandrel. Chalk it up to experience.

The bead release is primarily clay, so don't get it in your plumbing. After you've finished rinsing all your beads, let the water container sit so that the clay settles to the bottom, then pour off the clear water and wipe out the release.

Making Bead Shapes

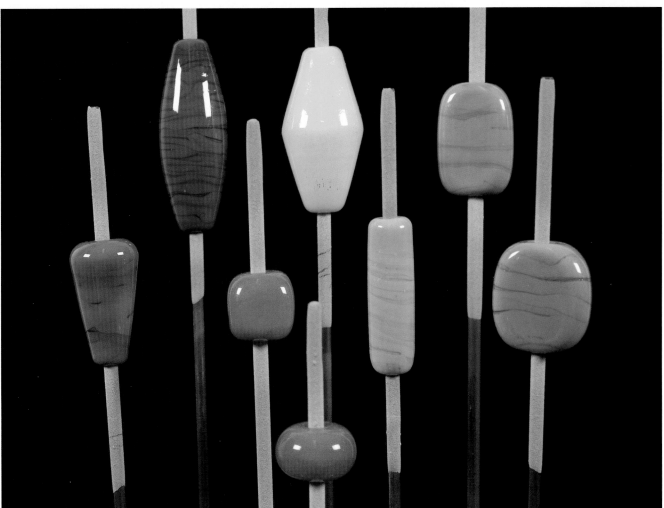

Once you have mastered the basic skills and the steps for making a round shape, you can begin creating other kinds of beads. In this chapter, you will learn how to make several different shapes that the projects later in this book will build upon.

To create a cylinder, make a complete wind of glass around your mandrel.

Continue winding the glass down the mandrel, with each wrap touching the last one, until the footprint is as wide as you want or you run out of hot glass.

Keep the mandrel just below the flame and the rod through the flame, and be sure each wrap touches the previous one. The glass must be hot enough to fuse to the previous wrap or you will get air bubbles.

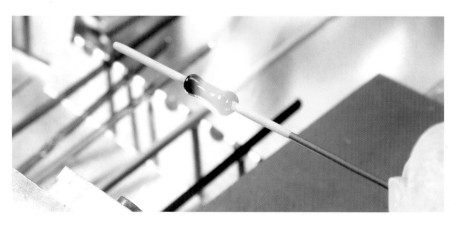

When you have finished making all the wraps, heat the glass bead.

Gently roll the bead on the graphite paddle, or marver, to shape it. Don't get the glass too hot, or surface tension will pull it up into the center, leaving the ends jagged. If this happens, heat the glass again and roll it on the paddle to get it back to a cylinder shape.

Have the mandrel rolling before you touch it to the paddle, and keep it level when rolling on the paddle. I like to make sure the part of the bead nearest my hand is perfectly centered, and then use this as a guide for the rest of the bead when rolling the mandrel. Don't press hard, and continue rolling as you lift it off. If the bead is not even, heat the glass and roll again until it is.

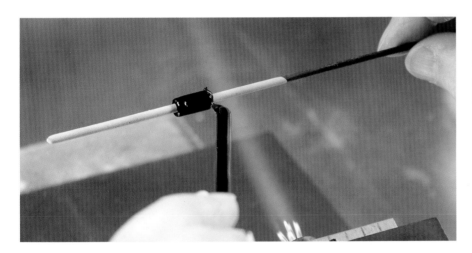

Now look at the end of the bead nearest your hand. This is the hardest end to get even, so work on it before you continue.

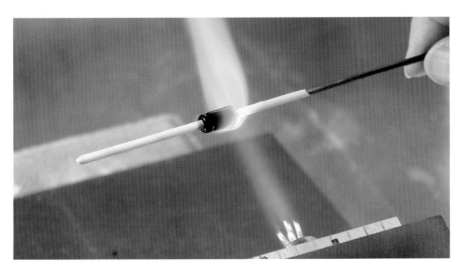

Heat just a tiny bit of the glass rod, touch it to the edge where more glass is needed, then pull and burn off the rod. Heat the bead and roll.

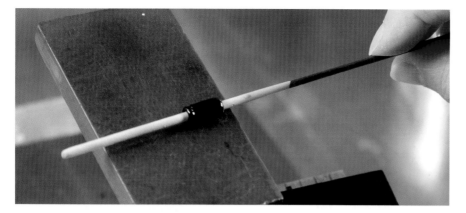

Continue until this end is even. Then get the footprint as long as you want, and make the other end even. The more evenly you add glass to your bead, the faster you will be able to get a balanced bead.

If you want a thicker cylinder, heat the rod and add the hot glass by touching it to the cylinder and rolling it away from you.

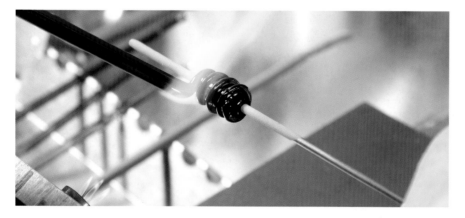

Heat again.

Roll the bead on the paddle until it is even and smooth. Check both ends to be sure they are even.

Tips

- Before using a mandrel, make sure it is straight, because you can't make a balanced bead on a bent mandrel. Roll it on the table or torch marver to check for wobbles (see the photo below).
- I find it easier to control rolling the bead by holding up the paddle. If you roll the bead on the marver on your bench, it can be difficult to see what is happening.
- Keep the entire length of the bead warm. While you are working on one end, occasionally warm up the other end, or it will thermal shock. If you suspect it is too cool, introduce it into the flame slowly from the outer part of the flame.

- If the footprint of the bead is at least as wide as the flame, it's easier to keep the bead ends neat.
- When making a tab bead (see page 50), the bead must be even and balanced before squashing it, or the result will be uneven. I find it helpful to switch hands to check if the bead is even. When I work, I normally hold the mandrel in my right hand, so I switch and hold it in my left hand, constantly turning. By looking at the bead both ways, it's easier for me to see if one end is thicker than the other.

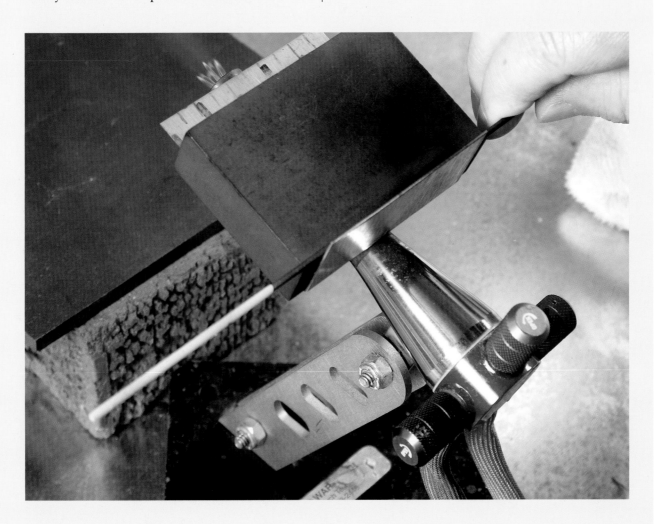

To make a cone or bicone shape, first make a cylinder bead.

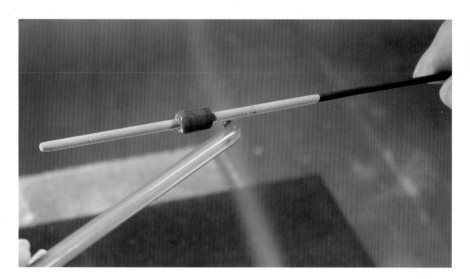

If the top end is not even, add a tiny bit of glass, then heat and marver it.

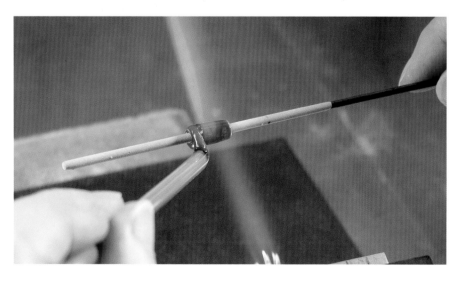

Now add wraps of glass to make the bead the length you want.

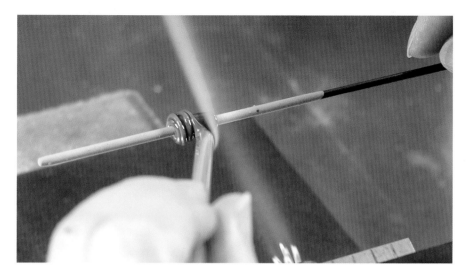

Add more wraps to the bottom to make that end thicker.

Heat the glass and roll it on the paddle at an angle. By adjusting the angle at which you are rolling, you can control the slant of the cone.

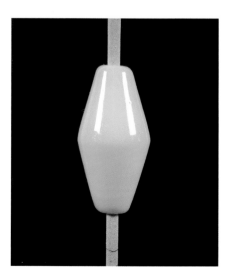

A bicone bead is simply two cone shapes put together, with the thickest ends in the middle of the bead. The easiest method is to make a cylinder, add glass at the center, heat it, and roll first at one slant, and then the other.

A barrel-shaped bead resembles a wooden barrel shape.
   Start by making a cylinder.

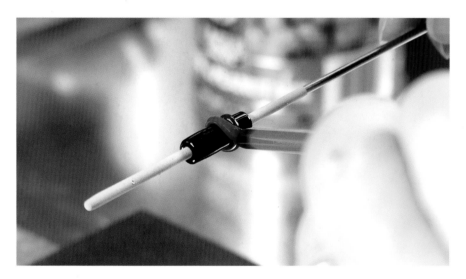

Then add glass at the center.

Heat and marver, using a gentle touch.

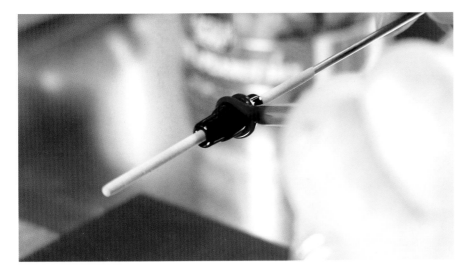

Keep adding glass and marvering until the center is the thickness you want.

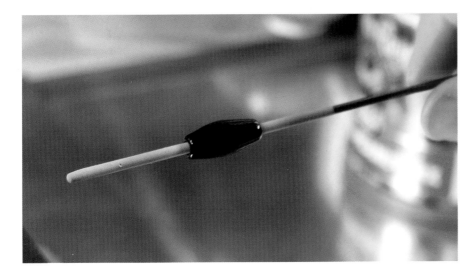

The barrel can have a long, gentle taper or be more pronounced, depending on what you want.

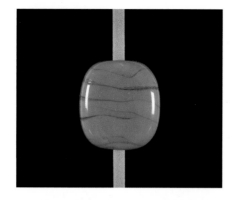
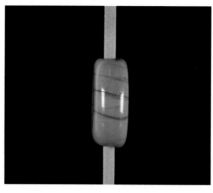

A tabular, or tab, bead has two flat surfaces created by squashing the bead. The final shape of the tab bead depends on the shape of the bead before it was squashed.

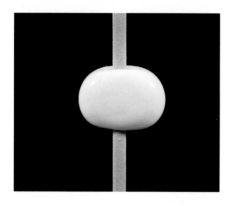

A short fat cylinder bead will make a squashed square bead. A round bead will make a squashed bead that is very tall.

A long cylinder will make a long tab bead. A barrel bead will make an elegant tapered tab bead.

Begin by making a cylinder and heat it evenly.

Bring it up to eye level, place it inside the squashers and press gently.

Don't press too hard; there should be at least one mandrel thickness of glass on each side of the mandrel. Then quickly flip it over and squash in the opposite direction, as squashers are seldom truly parallel.

After squashing, if you look closely, you can see concentric circles on the flat surfaces. These are chill marks from the metal. Fire-polish them by simply using the flame to melt them out. Don't heat the bead too much, or it will begin to round up. You are trying to melt and smooth just the surface of the bead.

Now look at the shape. If it needs adjusted a little, heat up that edge and nudge it with your paddle. Work until the shape is even.

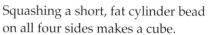

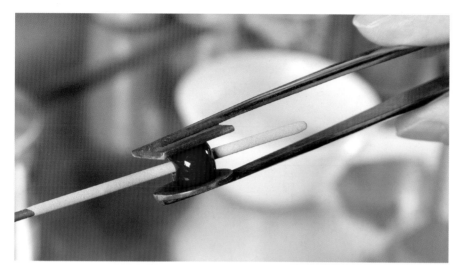

Squashing a short, fat cylinder bead on all four sides makes a cube.

Do a gentle squash first, flip over and squash again.

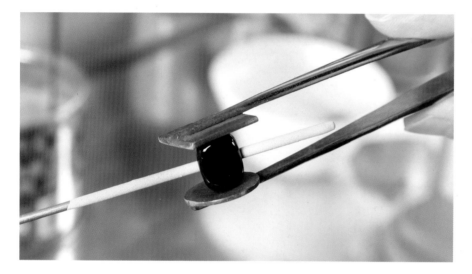

Then do the other two sides.

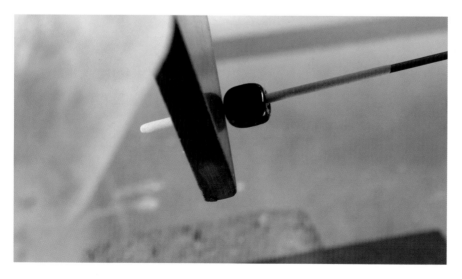

If the sides slumped out, you can heat and gently nudge them in with a paddle, being careful to not disturb the bead release.

To make a rectangle, make a cylinder bead and then squash on four sides. Don't forget to fire polish the flat surfaces.

Projects

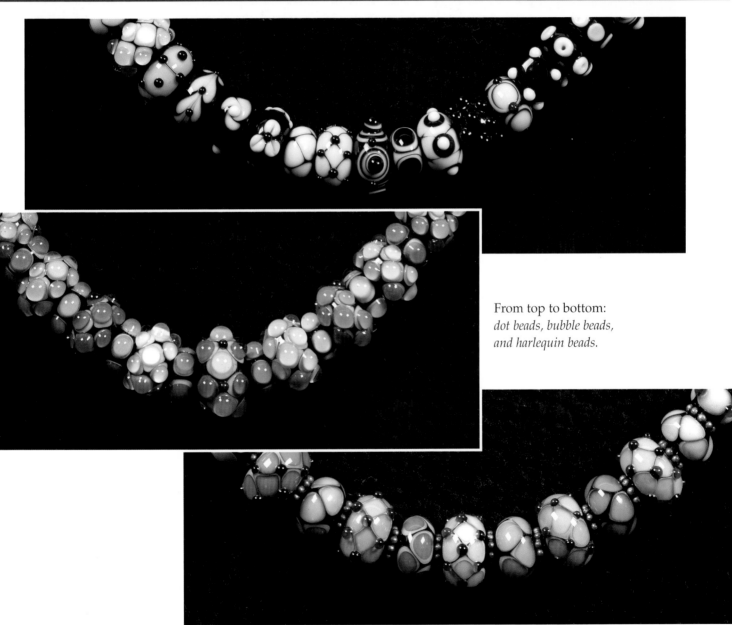

From top to bottom:
*dot beads, bubble beads,
and harlequin beads.*

This chapter presents twenty-two bead projects you can make, using the basic shapes and skills you have learned. Try some or all of these, and then experiment to create your own.

Dots are the basis for many decorative techniques. All of the patterns on the beads in the black and white strand on the previous page were made using dots. Besides the methods I explain here, there are many ways of applying dots, so try out different techniques and see what works for you. I usually use a rod of glass to apply dots, but if I want tiny dots, then I use a stringer. A good way to learn how to apply dots is to make a small, round bead as a base bead, and then add dots of the same color. That way, if you mess up, you can melt the dots in and start over without having to make the base bead again.

Be sure you're happy with the shape and size of your base bead before adding dots, since only the surface should be heated when dots are added. The end of the rod of glass should be neat. The base bead must be rigid and positioned below the flame to keep it warm.

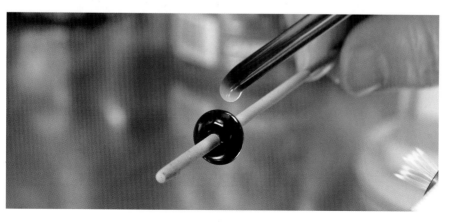

Keep turning it until you are ready to add the dots. Heat up the glass rod, but don't let it form a large gather unless you want a large dot. The larger the gather, the larger the footprint will be. When you are ready to add a dot, move the base bead over and move the rod out of the flame.

Touch the tip to the base bead. (If you use the side of the rod to add the dot, you will have a difficult time controlling the size and placement.) Pay attention to how hard you push the rod against the bead, because you want to replicate this. Pull the rod just slightly, and move it back into the flame to cut it off.

Don't pull very much, or you will end up with thin strings of glass that can fall back onto the bead, ruining the design.

By pulling just a little, the glass thins out just above the dot, and when put back into the flame, the thinnest part will melt first, flame-cutting the rod. If the rod gets rigid before the flame cuts it, resist the urge to pull; aim the flame where you want to cut it. Then heat just the dot to round it out, and move on to the next dot. Note that the dot was added outside the flame, not in it.

Continue adding dots as desired.

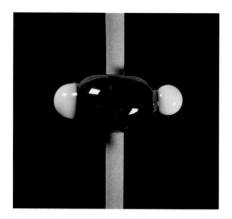

Raised dots should be mountains, not globes. Mountains are firmly attached to the base bead, but globes are not and can pop off. If you have a globe, heat just that dot until it melts into a mountain. Heat it a few seconds, take it out of the flame to check it, then heat again if needed. The glass in the dot can continue to move even out of the flame, which makes it easy to melt it too much, so go slowly. I used to put all the dots on a bead and then go back to make sure they were mountains, but now I check after each dot is added. Do whatever works best for you.

The position of your arms and hands is important. Rest the forearm of your hand holding the glass rod against the bench edge to steady it. Hold the glass rod and mandrel as close to the working ends as you can. If you are holding them too far out, they will be difficult to control. The size of the flame is important, too. When using a glass rod and making large dots, you can use a full flame, but when making smaller dots, turn down the flame.

When you are making a bead with three rows of dots, it's a good idea to do the middle row first, then the row closest to your hand, then the last row. It's easier to space the middle dots evenly and then base the position of the other rows on those. The row closest to your hand is always the most difficult. Angle the mandrel down so that you can use the tip of the rod, then put the dots on the other side of the middle row.

The shape and size of a dot depend on the shape and size of its footprint, the size of the glass rod, how much glass is molten, how hard you press, the shape of the base bead, and neighboring dots. Dots on a cylinder bead will become ovals when melted in, and large dots on a small, round bead won't remain round either.

If a dot isn't quite large enough, you can carefully add more glass to it. If a dot is too big, heat it and then touch it with a cool rod of glass. Pull the rod away, which will pull some of the glass from the dot, and flame-cut it. Be careful to not flame-cut it too far out, or what is left will fall back onto the bead. Then carefully melt the dot into a round shape. There are many ways to evenly space dots on a bead, all of which take practice. When you are putting four dots on a small bead, try the horizon method.

Make the first dot.

Turn the bead until that dot is on the horizon, and add the second dot on line with the mandrel.

Turn again until that dot is on the horizon, add the third dot, and turn again for the fourth dot.

This does take some practice, but once you get the hang of it, it's a good way to put four evenly spaced dots on a bead. For three evenly spaced dots, turn the bead until the first dot is just over the horizon, add the second dot, and repeat for the third dot.

Here's another way to evenly space dots.

Put the first dot down, and then point the mandrel toward you to add a second dot opposite the first one. You are dividing the space in half, and then you can divide each half into two or three sections. This method works for many beadmakers, but I have trouble getting the second dot on the equator of the bead, so I seldom do it this way.

Here's a technique for larger beads.

Simply start adding dots and continue until you are almost all the way around. Then turn the bead to see how much space is left.

Judge whether to add two or three more dots. Err on the lesser side.

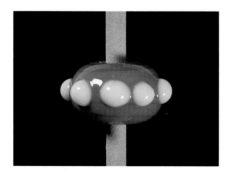

Crowded dots will appear as a mistake more than a little extra space between dots will. It's not important that the spacing be precise. I am happy if it just looks precise! With practice, when adding a lot of dots, you will develop a rhythm, which is important.

 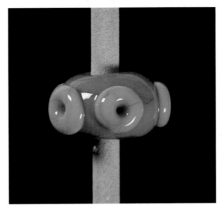

Dots can be flattened with a paddle or any other flat tool.

Make a base bead and add dots.

Then heat just one dot.

Press it with a flat tool. Don't get the dot too hot, or it will melt into the base bead.

Continue around the bead. This can also be useful to enlarge a footprint that is a little too small.

As a further decorative technique, you can heat each flattened dot and poke it with a thin mandrel or pick, or you can poke each dot without flattening it. If your tool gets too hot, it will stick to the glass, so put it in the water after several pokes to cool it. If it gets stuck in the glass, resist the urge to pull. Wait for the glass to cool a little, and you can usually wiggle the tool loose.

Layered dots have concentric circles of colors like a bull's-eye.

Make a row of dots on a base bead, leaving some room between them, because they will spread. Turn and heat evenly to melt them in.

Now add dots of another color in their center.

Melt this row in. As the dots melt, they will push the first color out.

Continue for as many circles as you want. Just be sure to melt in each row slowly and evenly before adding another color.

You can leave the last row of dots raised, add tiny dots—the possibilities are endless!

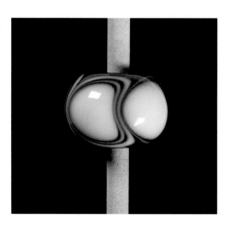

If the bead gets too hot, the dots can slide, ruining their round shape. You want to heat the surface of the bead, not the whole bead itself.

To stack the dots, don't melt them in. Add a slightly smaller dot of a new color on top of each dot, making sure it is firmly attached to the previous one. As the stack of dots gets higher, it will tend to lean, which can make a very interesting bead. If you don't want the stack to lean, as you add each dot, turn the bead so that the stack hangs straight down until the glass becomes rigid.

To create this complex-looking bead, you add rows of dots to a cylinder base bead. For the dots, I like to use one opaque color of glass and three or four shades of a transparent color, starting with the lightest one at the top and continuing with darker shades on each row, creating a gradation of color.

Make sure both ends of the cylinder are even, and marver.

Add a row of dots around the top using an opaque color, and melt in gently.

Add a transparent colored dot on top of every opaque dot in the first row.

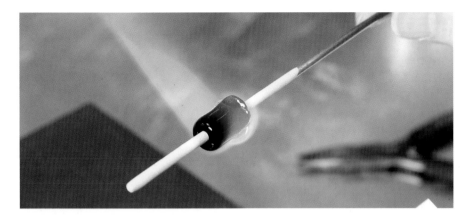

Melt in.

Marver gently so that the dots don't slide.

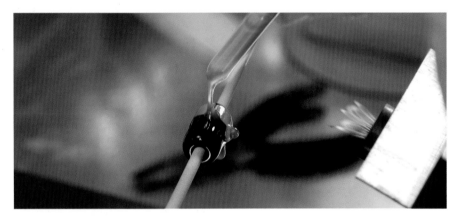

Using the opaque color, add a second row of dots between the dots in the first row and about halfway covering them.

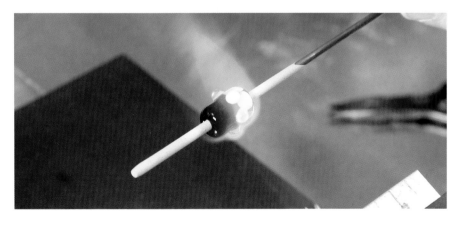

Melt in.

Put a transparent color on top of each dot in the second row, and melt in.

Marver gently.

Add a third row of opaque dots between and about halfway covering the second row of dots, and melt in.

Put a transparent color on top and melt in, marvering gently. Continue down the cylinder.

This technique also works well on a round bead, although there isn't room for as many rows.

Stringers are thin rods of glass used for decorating beads and for adding tiny dots. You can make stringers from any color of glass, but because white glass is softer, white stringers are difficult to use. There are several ways to make a stringer. I usually use tweezers or pliers.

Heat up the end of a glass rod and get a gather. Hold the rod overhand and angle it up to balance the gather on the end.

Take it out of the flame and wait a few seconds, then grab a tiny bit of the gather with tweezers or pliers.

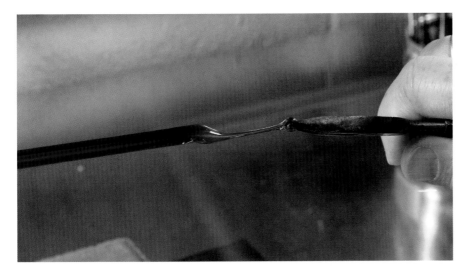

Slowly pull. If you want a thicker stringer, wait longer for the glass to cool and pull slower.

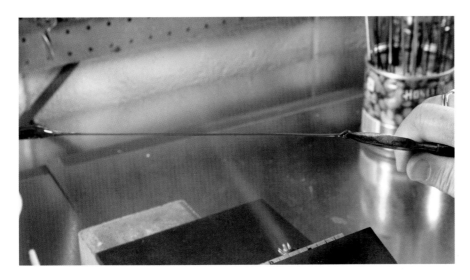

You will feel the glass become rigid. Hold it taut for a few seconds to allow the glass time to cool and set up.

Then either flame-cut it off the rod or use tweezers or pliers to thermal shock it off. This method results in a small tail on one end.

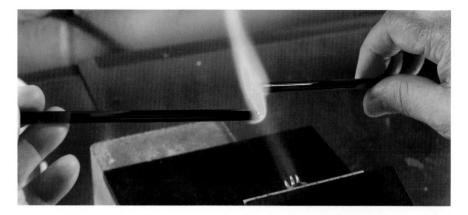

Another technique is to use two rods of the same color. Heat up both ends.

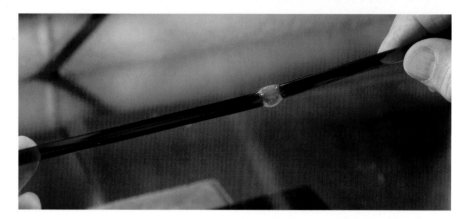

Press them together in the flame until you have a small football shape.

Take the glass out of the flame, wait a few seconds, and then pull slowly. Again, hold it taut until it sets up.

Flame-cut one end off the rod, hold the stringer with tweezers, and flame-cut or thermal shock the other rod off.

The trick to getting good stringers is to wait those few seconds before pulling, and then pull slowly. Most beginners get the glass too hot and pull too fast, resulting in very thin stringers that are impossible to use. Stringers longer than 12 inches are difficult to use, so make shorter ones. Experience will teach you how hot the glass should be and how large of a gather to make. Once the gather reaches a certain size, it is much easier to control by holding the rod overhand and aiming the end up.

If you get halfway through making a bead and realize you need a stringer you don't have, you can make an emergency stringer.

While you are keeping your bead warm, heat up a glass rod. When the gather is large enough, heat the end of the mandrel and touch it with the hot glass rod.

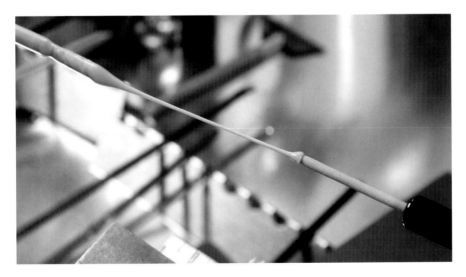

Pull a stringer. Work quickly, since your bead is now out of the flame and cooling off. Don't pull too hard, or the end of the stringer will pull off the mandrel. When the stringer is rigid, burn off the rod. Then use your tweezers to hold the stringer, and pull or burn it off the mandrel. Return your bead to the flame to rewarm it. The stringer will cool off quickly, and then you can continue with your bead.

Here's how to use the stringers you have made to decorate your beads. After you have made your base bead and let it get rigid, hold it under the flame and turn to keep it warm.

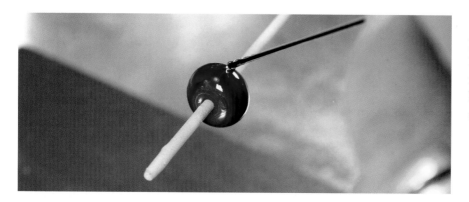

Now turn the flame down a bit. Hold the stringer at the side of the flame to melt just the tip, move the bead and stringer out of the flame and attach the stringer to the bead.

Now move the bead and stringer back to the side of the flame, coming close enough to the flame to soften the stringer. Aim to keep the stringer in one position and move the bead to "write" with it, which is the opposite of your inclination. You can leave the stringer raised or melt it in.

If you are leaving it raised, make sure it is firmly attached.

This definitely takes a lot of practice. Note that all the work is done to the side of the flame, not in it. A stringer thinner than $1/16$ inch will melt too fast and get out of control, so work with a thicker stringer.

To make a really thin black line on a bead, make a stringer using a black filigrana rod. When you pull the stringer, the black line gets really thin, and your eyes will not notice the clear around it when it is on the bead.

In this project, you'll make bubble or eye beads with three rows of dots.

First make a base bead and then add a row of large dots in an opaque color around the diameter.

Keep enough space between dots; don't get them too close, or they will merge when melted in.

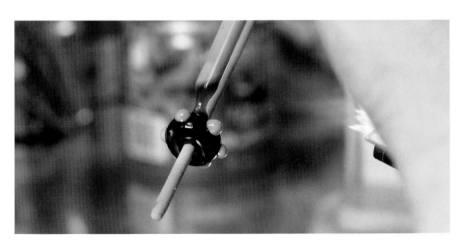

Now add another row of dots on the side closest to your hand, putting them between the middle dots.

Then add a similar row on the other side.

Melt all the dots evenly. Let the bead become rigid, but keep turning it, and heat up a transparent color.

When ready to add the transparent color, move the base bead to the side of the flame, move the rod to the side of the flame, and then touch it to the center of a dot, pushing relatively hard. Pull it up slightly and burn it off. The glass dot should be hot enough to slump into a rounded mound. If not, put it in the flame and get it round, but not so hot that it melts into the base.

Now heat the rod again and continue.

Do the middle row first, the row nearest your hand next, and then the outside row.

If there is enough room, you can add tiny dots between the larger dots. For this, use a stringer that you made beforehand.

Turn the flame down, and heat just the tip of the stringer near the flame, not in it. It will melt very fast, so be careful.

When a small amount of glass is hot, touch it between the dots, and flame-cut it.

Then hit the dot with the flame to round it up. Continue around the bead.

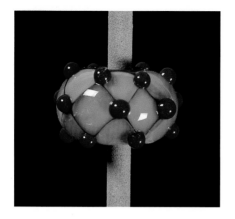

The classic harlequin bead depends on neighboring dots to create a square and triangle pattern. Dots in the center row become squares with a triangle on each side when melted smooth. This bead is similar to the bubble bead, but here the large dots are melted smooth, and there are three rows of tiny raised dots. Start by making a base bead.

Let it get rigid, and then add a row of dots around the diameter, keeping sufficient space between them.

Add a second row on the side closest to your hand between those dots.

Add a third row on the other side.

Melt these dots in evenly. If you spaced the dots correctly, they will form a harlequin pattern as they melt.

Now add a color, usually transparent, on top of the first dots and melt in.

To finish the bead, turn down the flame and use a stringer to add tiny dots, usually of the base color, at the corners of the squares.

Do the middle row first, the side nearest your hand next, and then the other side. It may take some practice to make the original dots the correct size and the right distance apart. If they are too large, they will merge when you melt them. If they are too small, they won't get close enough to form the pattern.

Masked dots are made by partially overlapping dots of one color with dots of the base color.

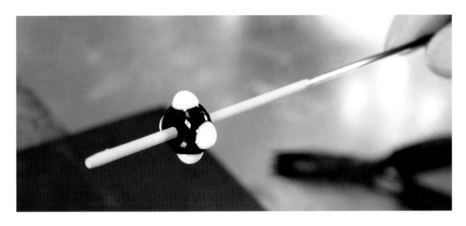

First make a base bead in an opaque color. Add dots of another opaque color around the diameter of the base bead, and melt them in.

Then add dots of the first color on top of the second color, placing them off center so that one edge touches the base bead.

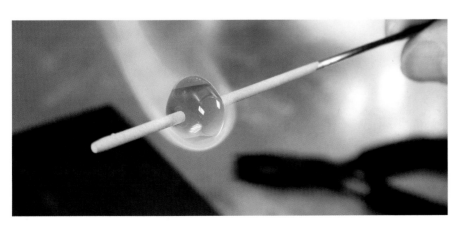

Now melt them in, and the second color will become crescents. This simple technique can create very complex patterns, so experiment.

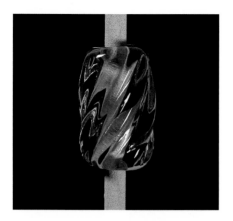

Many surfaces can be used to create patterns on your glass bead. To make a groovy bead, use an aluminum plate with grooves in it, available from most lampworking supply companies. Transparent glass is especially good for this bead, allowing you to see the pattern on the front and back of the bead at the same time.

Start by making a thick cylinder bead.

Heat it evenly.

Then quickly roll it across the grooved pattern. Don't push too hard, or the grooves will be too deep, causing the bead to crack. Don't get the bead too hot, or rolling it will misshape it. You can roll the bead straight across or angle the plate for a diagonal pattern.

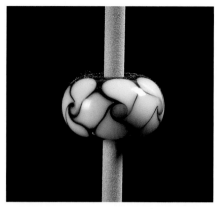

To create twisted dots or patterns, you will need a thick stringer, so make one beforehand and set it aside. Any pattern of dots or lines can be twisted. To create the black and white bead, I twisted the center junction of dots in a harlequin pattern. Using a lime green stringer to twist the dots left tiny dots of that color.

To twist three dots into flower petals, first make a base bead.

Then place three groups of three opaque dots around the bead. If the base bead is large enough, the groups can have more dots. An uneven number like three or five makes a more interesting flower than an even number.

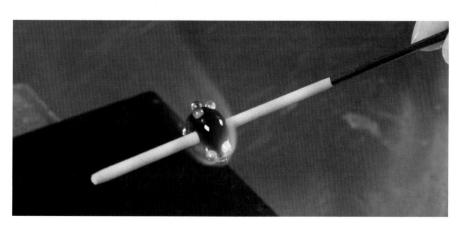

For my example, I am using a base dot of white, which gets clear when it is hot. Notice the spacing of the three dots. If they are too close, they will merge when melted. If they are too far apart, they won't form a flower design.

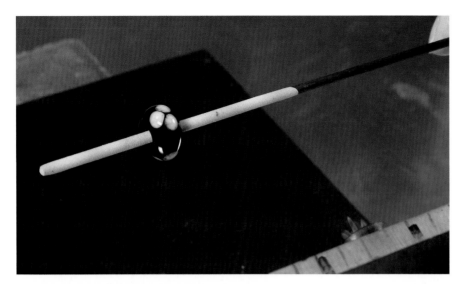

Melt them evenly. To create more depth, you can add a dot of a transparent color on top of each white dot. Melt them also, and let the bead get rigid.

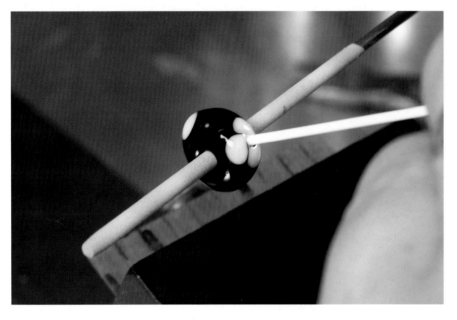

Then, one by one, heat just the center of each of the three dots, remove from the flame, put the end of the stringer into the center, and gently twist. Depending on how hot the glass is, you may need to wait a few seconds before twisting. Now snap the stringer off. If it bends when you try to snap it off, it is still too hot. Blowing on it will cool it quickly so that you can snap it off, but be careful not to get the hot glass too close to your lips. Quickly return the bead to the flame to warm it up, and then continue with the next group of dots.

The stringer will leave a small dot of color when you snap it off. If you don't want this dot to show, use a stringer the color of the base bead or add a raised dot for the center. After twisting, the surface of the bead will no longer be smooth. You can either leave it as it is or carefully melt the surface until it is smooth.

To create a raised petal design, start by making a base bead.

Add three groups of three opaque dots for the petals, taking care with the spacing.

Now heat just one dot, and press a knife or any other sharp tool down its center to create a crease.

Let this petal cool a little, and repeat for the other petals. If the petals get too hot, the creases will melt, so do one petal of each group, then a second petal of each group, and so on.

Add a dot of another color in the center if you wish. This technique also works well for creating raised leaves.

Another flower design can be made by pulling petals.

First make a base bead, in this case a cylinder, although any shape can be used.

Then add opaque dots for the petals, melting them in. A group of three or five dots makes a nice flower. Space the flower around.

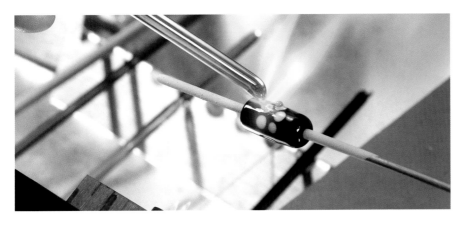

Adding a transparent dot on top of the opaque dots creates more depth.

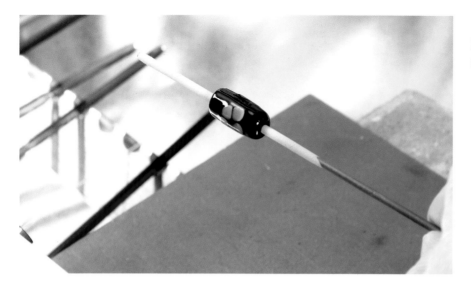

Heat all the dots smooth, and wait for the glass to become rigid.

Now heat the outside edge of a dot. Put a rake or poke with a sharp point into the outside edge of the dot, and pull the glass out from the center of the petal. Do this out of the flame, not in it.

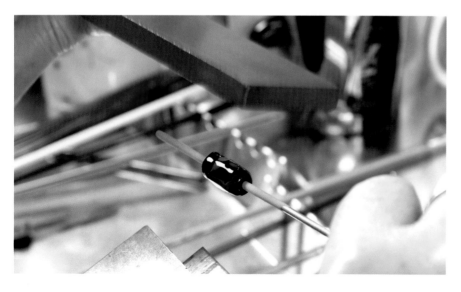

If you put the rake just outside the dot and pull, you will create a pointed petal, as shown. If you put it just inside the dot, the petal will have a rounded tip. Continue raking each dot to create the petals. All this raking will distort the shape of your bead, so gently heat and paddle it back into shape. To finish, put a white dot in the center of each flower.

Many patterns can be created by raking.

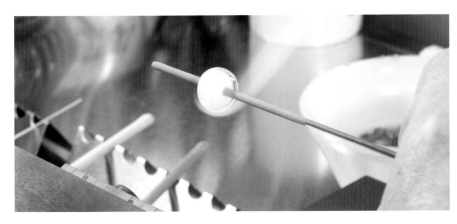

First make a base bead large enough that the surface can be heated without heating the whole bead.

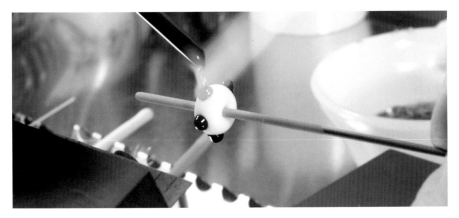

Place a row of dots around the center.

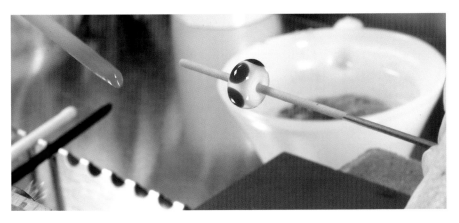

Melt them in.

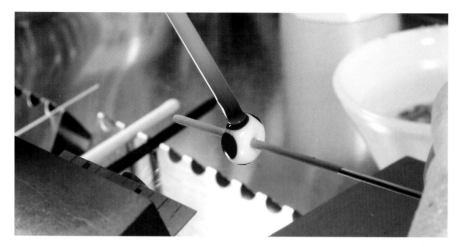

Add opaque or transparent dots on top of the first set of dots.

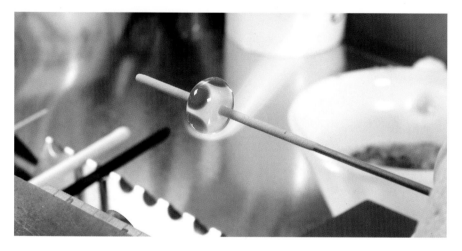

Melt them in and let the bead get rigid. Now place the bead in the top of the flame, turning the mandrel away from you so that the bottom of the bead is coming up out of the flame. As you turn the bead, watch for its surface to get molten. If the glass isn't hot enough, keep turning it until it is. Once it is molten, put the rake just on the surface and continue turning.

Hold the rake just above the flame, not in it. Keep the rake on the surface of the bead, as it grabs and pulls some of the glass with it. Just the bottom of the bead should be in the flame, or the whole bead will get too hot and move with the rake, distorting the shape.

If the rake sticks in the bead, wait a few seconds, and then wiggle it to break it loose. If glass is stuck to the rake, you can shatter it off by heating it in the flame for a few seconds and then putting it in your water dish.

Experiment with different patterns. Try laying down lines of stringers and raking through them. Layering colors can create interesting shading.

Making twisties is really good practice for learning to read the heat in the glass. Choose your colors carefully—they need to be strong contrasting colors. You will be pulling the glass into thin rods, so don't use all transparent colors, because they tend to become too pale. There are always surprises, so experiment with colors. Use long rods, because short ones won't give you enough of a handle when twisting.

To make a two-color twisty, choose two colors.

Hold one rod in each hand in an overhand position, and heat ¾ to 1 inch of one end of each rod. The rods need to be hot enough to stick together, but don't let them start to droop.

Now place the heated end of the two rods together with 3/4 to 1 inch overlapping. If the ends of the rods curl up, heat and press them down on your marver.

Turn this overlap in the flame to heat it into a football shape, and keep turning to heat it evenly. Don't pull. The glass has a tendency to pull apart as you are turning, so to counter that, slightly push the rods together. One hand may have the tendency to turn faster than the other, so watch for that, and don't start to twist yet. Take the rods out of the flame occasionally to allow the heat time to sink into the center of the glass, and keep turning.

When the line between the two colors disappears and you have a nice football shape, evenly heat it, take it out of the flame, and wait a few seconds. Then pull and twist. You must twist in opposite directions, but luckily that seems to be a natural way to do it.

Once you start twisting, there is no going back, so twist as fast as you can. Don't pull too much, or the twisty will be too thin to use. The glass will let you know when to stop—it will become harder and harder to twist. At that point, hold it taut and wait a few seconds to allow the glass to harden, and then burn off one handle.

Hold the twisty with tweezers and burn off the other handle, or use pliers to thermal shock it off. The twisty will take longer to cool than a stringer, as it is thicker, so be patient.

As a last step, heat the ends of the rods, and use tweezers to pluck off any remaining twists of color.

To make a three-color twisty, choose three colors. Decide which color will be in the center, and warm about 1 inch of the end.

Heat the second color, and lay a thick line of glass along the end of the first rod, $3/4$ to 1 inch long.

Think of a line of toothpaste. Try to make the overlapped section at least as long as the flame is wide. Then burn off the second rod. If the glass gets too hot and droops, touch it to the marver to cool it off—don't let it sag.

Now take the third color, heat it, and lay a thick line of the same length on the opposite side of the first rod.

When the third rod reaches the end of the first rod, pull it down a little so that it lines up horizontally with the center color.

Then heat and turn until you have a football shape. Push together slightly so that the rods don't pull apart, and don't twist. Because the handles are thinner than the center section, they will heat faster and will pull while you are trying to pull and twist the center section, so try to keep them cooler. Don't let the football get too hot. While turning, take it out of the flame occasionally to allow the heat time to sink into the center of the glass.

When the football is evenly heated, take out of the flame, wait a few seconds, and then pull and twist.

Burn off the two ends as for the two-color twisty, and clean the ends of the glass rods.

To create a Christmas tree bead, first make a two- or three-color twisty.

Then using transparent green glass, make a cone-shaped bead.

Heat only the tip of the twisty, and attach it to the top of the cone. The surface of the bead needs to be warm enough for the twisty to stick.

Work with the twisty held just under the flame, where it is easy to adjust the heat by coming up a little into the flame or down a little out of it. As it softens, press it down and around the cone. You should be pressing the twisty onto the surface, not just laying it on, but don't press too hard or the twisty could snap.

When you reach the bottom, burn the twisty off. Reheat the entire bead to make sure the glass is well attached, with no undercuts.

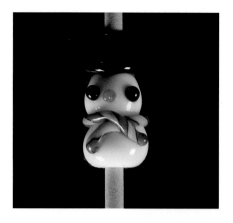

To create a bead that looks like a cute snowman, first make a two- or three-color twisty for his scarf, a black stringer for his eyes, and an orange stringer for his carrot nose. If you use the same twisty you used for the tree, they will make a nice pair. There are several steps to make the different components of the snowman. It's important to keep turning the snowman the entire time you are making him, keeping him all warm.

Start the snowman by making a short, black cylinder for his hat.

Wind white glass on the mandrel, making sure it touches the black.

Then marver it into a cone shape. Make this about as long as you want his body to be.

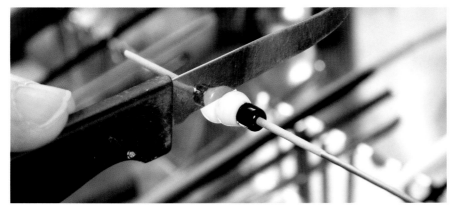

Heat the center of the white glass, and roll it against a paring knife or similar tool to make a crease between the head and body. Don't saw with the knife or press too hard; if the glass becomes too thin, it will crack. Just roll the glass against the knife. Usually you will need to add a little white glass to even out the bottom.

When it is even, heat up just the bottom of the snowman, being careful to not lose the crease, and hold the mandrel vertically. Gravity will pull the glass down, making a nice puckered hole.

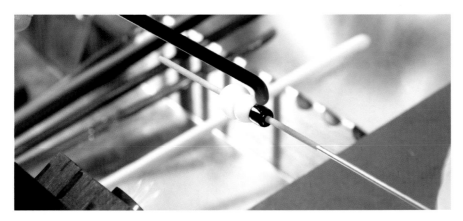

To add the brim on the hat, heat up a thin rod of black, but don't let it form a gather. Touch it lightly to the bottom of the hat.

Slowly roll the mandrel, pulling the glass around into a brim.

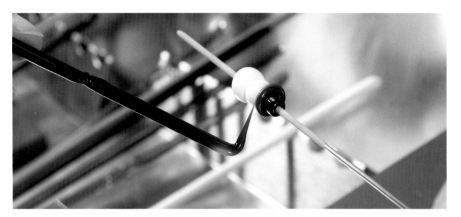

When you reach the beginning, pull the rod to thin out the glass, and burn it off. Carefully heat the brim to melt any lines in; don't get it too hot, or the brim will melt into the hat.

To add the scarf, heat just the tip of the twisty, and anchor it on the body.

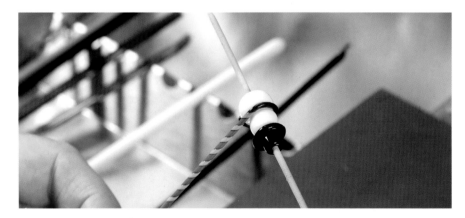

Hold the twisty and snowman just under the flame, and as the twisty softens, push it up, around his neck, and down to form the other end.

Burn the twisty off, and reheat the scarf to be sure it is attached well.

To make the eyes, heat just the tip of the black stringer, touch it to one side of the face, and then burn it off. Repeat for the other eye, keeping them far enough apart to add the nose between them. Be sure both dots are mountains, not globes. Add more black or take some away as necessary to get the eyes about the same size.

Now make the nose by heating the tip of the orange stringer and touching it between the eyes. Pull and burn off.

If you didn't get a carrot shape, heat the nose, barely touch it with the cooled stringer, and pull just a little. Burn off the stringer. A nose that is too long can easily be knocked off, so it's best to hit it with the flame a little to shorten it, but try to keep that carrot shape.

If the nose gets too close to the scarf, heat the nose and use a razor blade tool to press it up a little.

Frit is crushed glass. You can buy it in various sizes or make your own. *Warning*: Making and working with frit can release small particles of glass into the air, which are hazardous to breathe. Always wear a respirator, make sure your ventilation is good, and avoid sprinkling or pouring frit. Gently spooning it puts less glass into the air.

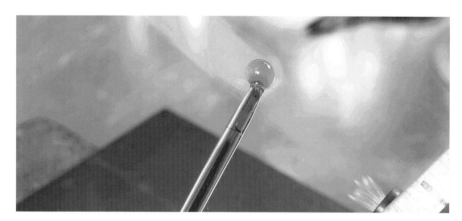

To make frit, heat the end of a rod into a gather, holding it upward to help balance the gather.

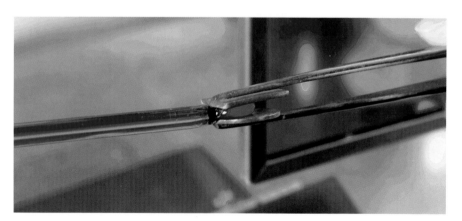

Then squash it as thin as you can.

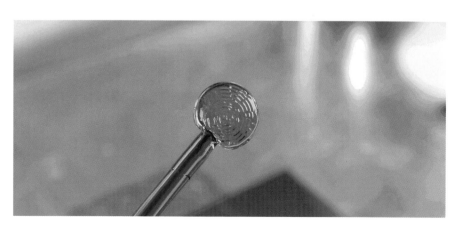

The metal of the squashers makes chill marks on the glass, which you can easily see. Immediately plunge it into a clean bowl of cold water, and the glass will shatter into small pieces.

To dry it, pour the water out of the bowl, taking care not to get any glass down the drain, and scrape the frit onto a paper towel. Place in the sun or on top of a warm kiln, and it will quickly dry. Store in a small, clean container marked with the COE and color. I use watch cases to store my frits, but film canisters work well too. You can mix colors of different frits to make your own special combinations.

To use the frit on a bead, sprinkle it onto your marver. Make a base bead, and let it cool a little. Then heat just the surface, roll it in the frit, and melt it smooth. If you want to leave the surface pebbly, make sure the frit is firmly attached.

To put a heavy coating of frit on the bead, I like to use an inexpensive metal ashtray.

Bend it, put the frit in it, and then roll the hot bead in it.

A metal spoon is also handy for applying frit. Use these over a china saucer to catch stray frit. Brush the excess back into its container with a small brush.

One way to use frit is in making crackle beads. For this project, use Moretti new purple glass, #273, for your base bead. I have tried this technique with other colors, but none of them have worked as well as this purple. I am also using a silver green reduction frit but not reducing it. (See the next chapter for information on reduction frits.) *Warning*: Breathing glass dust is hazardous to your health. Before starting to work, read the warning in the previous project.

Make several thin stringers of intense black. Put a thin sprinkling of the green frit on your marver. I like to use the smooth side of my groovy aluminum marver, because I can lift it and move it around without disturbing the frit.

Now make a thick cylinder bead from the purple glass.

Get the cylinder hot, and roll it lightly across the frit.

Try to have a sparse, relatively even coating, and heat it enough to be sure it is attached to the bead. Don't worry about melting it smooth yet.

To make several wraps of the intense black stringer around the bead, first anchor the stringer at one end.

Make very loose wraps to the other end.

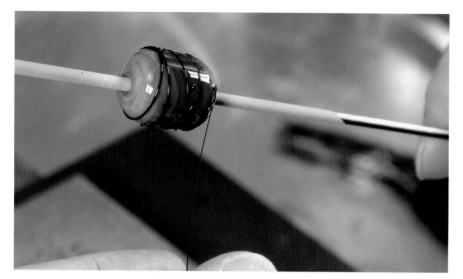

Then reverse direction, wrap back to the first end, and burn the stringer off. Because the stringer is thin, it is very hard to control, so work farther outside the flame. This is a random design, so don't worry about precision.

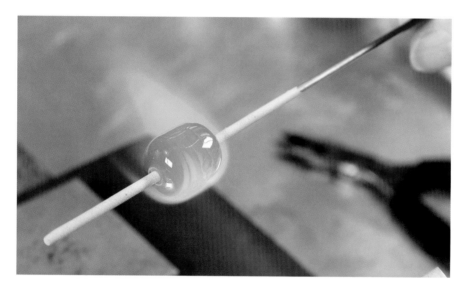

Now use one of my favorite techniques: Heat it up and really cook it. You should see the stringer break up into a matrix.

When you are happy with the pattern, spend some time shaping the bead into an even cylinder.

Then squash it.

Check and gently correct the shape of the bead, and fire-polish the chill marks.

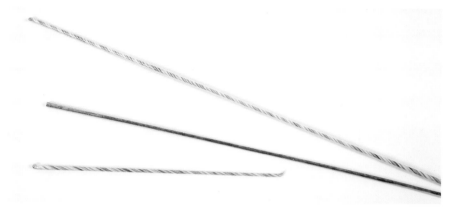

The reaction that occurs between silver foil or leaf and ivory glass can be used to make wonderful patterns in a bead. For this technique, foil works better than leaf, as it is thicker and gets more silver on the glass.

To make a silver stringer, first tear off a piece of silver foil about 1 x 1 inch, and lay it on your marver.

Warm the end of a dark ivory rod, getting it just hot enough to pick up the silver foil, and roll it across the foil.

Then use your tweezers or knife to burnish or rub it on the glass.

Now heat the end and get a gather.

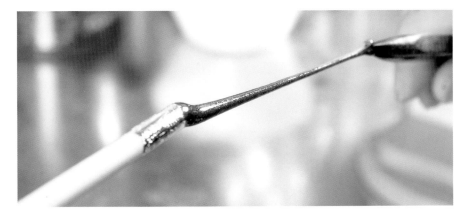

Pull out a thick stringer. Either burn it off the rod or use your pliers to thermal shock it off.

Continue heating the end and pulling it out into a stringer until all of the silver is gone. These stringers can be used on a bead as they are or be made into twisted silver stringers.

To make a twisted stringer, warm about 1 inch of the end of a dark ivory rod.

Lay down three or four lines of the silver stringer, about 1 inch long, around the ivory rod.

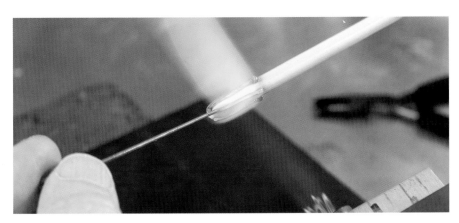

Keep the rod under the flame, not in it.

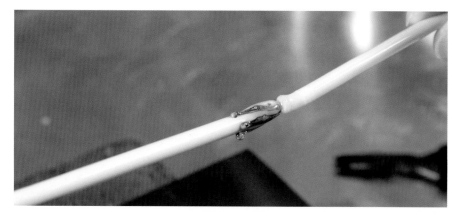

Heat another rod of any color, as it is only serving as a handle, and attach it to the end of the rod with the silver stringers.

Heat and turn the silvered section, pushing the two handles together slightly, until you have a football shape of hot glass.

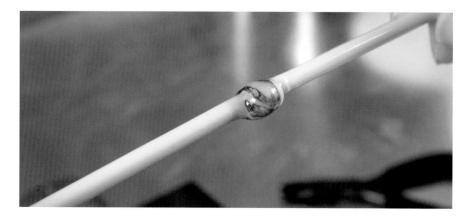

Take it out of the flame, wait a few seconds, and then twist and pull.

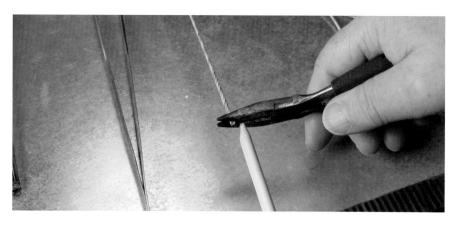

Burn off one handle, and thermal shock the other handle off. Heat and pull off any silver on the ends of the rods to have them ready for their next use.

You can use the twisted silver stringer you just made to create a batik bead. For this bead, I like to use a transparent glass (here a dark gray), although an opaque glass might be interesting too.

Begin by making a thick cylinder bead.

I added glass three times to get it thick enough.

Now heat just the tip of the twisted silver stringer, and anchor it to the bead.

Keeping the stringer on the edge or just outside the flame, and moving the bead and not the stringer, "write" with the stringer.

The silver stringer is more brittle than a plain glass stringer, so don't push it too hard, or it will snap. This is a good bead on which to practice writing with stringers, because the pattern is very organic and not precise.

Heat the bead, melt the stringer smooth, and check the shape of the bead.

Then heat and squash it. In my example, I am using my ice tongs to make a lentil-shaped bead.

Fire-polish the chill marks and do any final shaping. If an edge is a little off, heat it and gently nudge it into place with your paddle.

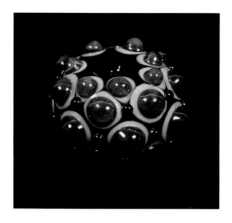 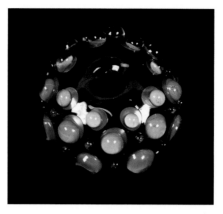 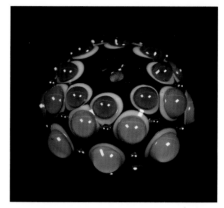

If you want large beads, they would be heavy if made from solid glass, so you can make them hollow. These beads take some practice, and there are several ways to make them. This project will teach you my favorite method. When you first make hollow beads, it can be hard to get the walls even, and if you use a light transparent glass, this is more evident, so use opaque glass until you improve.

Begin by making a thick stringer for the tiny dots, and set it aside. This bead uses a large amount of glass, so start with a full length of rod.

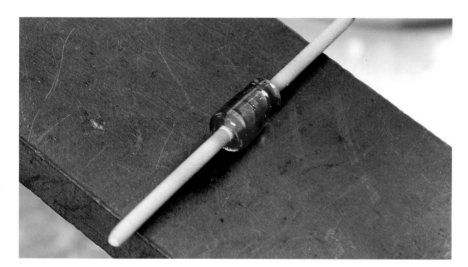

First make a thin cylinder and get the ends even. The length of the cylinder determines in part the size of the bead, so don't get it too long. Keep it under 1/2 inch until you have some experience.

Now start winding glass into a disk on one end of the cylinder. Have the rod molten so that it will fuse to the previous wrap. Keep the disks under the flame, or they will start to thicken and melt down.

After several wraps, burn off the rod, and start another disk on the other end of the cylinder. Aim to fuse each wrap to the previous one with no gaps.

Try to keep the thickness even and the disks at a round, even height.

Alternate the side you work on so that each disk stays warm as it builds higher, and warm the whole bead occasionally. The disks are relatively thin and will cool faster than a solid bead.

At first, build the disks straight up, and then start wrapping them toward each other.

I heat each disk down to the mandrel once in a while as insurance.

When they are almost touching, gently heat the edges, and nudge them together with a paddle. Be careful not to get the edges too hot, or they will thicken and slump.

When the edges are joined, gently heat the glass. Watch for holes, which will look like dark spots. As the bead is heated, the air inside will expand, and if there are any holes, the bead will collapse, so check carefully. Don't try to add glass to plug the holes—use your tweezers to pinch the glass together.

Heat the bead slowly, and don't let it get too hot. The glass moves differently than when making a solid bead, and it's very easy to lose control.

When the bead is a nice round shape, add dots around the middle with an opaque color, keeping then far enough apart to be able to add tiny dots between them later.

Then add a row of slightly smaller dots on each side of the middle row and between the dots, first on the side closer to your hand.

Then add them on the other side.

Go back to the first side and add another row of even smaller dots close to the mandrel, and then do the same on the other side.

Now melt all of these dots. Heat one side first and get the dots melting, and then move to the other side.

Once the sides are almost smooth, heat the center row. Don't try to melt all the dots at once; the bead will get too hot and flop off center, distorting the dots. Go slowly. If the sides get a little off center, use a paddle to coax the bead back into the correct shape.

Once the dots are melted smooth, heat a rod of a transparent glass and put a row of large raised dots around the middle row. I like to use a gradation of colors, with a light transparent color in the center and darker colors down the sides.

Next, put dots on each side of the middle row.

Then add the last, smallest row of dots nearest the mandrel. By alternating working on the sides, the bead stays warm.

As a last design element, use the stringer to put tiny dots between the larger dots around the middle.

Then add the dots between the next row on each side. Be sure that these dots are mountains, not globes. To finish, flame anneal the entire bead, and then put it in the kiln to anneal.

The final size and shape of the bead can be controlled by how far apart the two disks start, or how long the cylinder was made, and by how high each disk becomes. If the disks aren't high enough for the width of the bead, an olive shape will develop and the ends will be ragged. The shape also can be influenced by tilting the mandrel while the bead is hot, which will create a strawberry shape.

Another way to make hollow beads is to wind two disks on the mandrel with no cylinder between them. When I first started making hollow beads, I hated cleaning out the bead release because there were always some chips inside the bead. To avoid this problem, I started making the cylinder first and discovered that this also gives the disks a little more stability as you wind them up. To remove any pieces of bead release, squirt water into the completed bead with a syringe, and the bead release will swirl out with the water.

You can also make a bead within a bead using a similar technique. First make a small bead, and then build two disks beside, up, and over it, being careful that the disks don't touch it.

Surface Techniques, Inclusions, and Other Fun Stuff

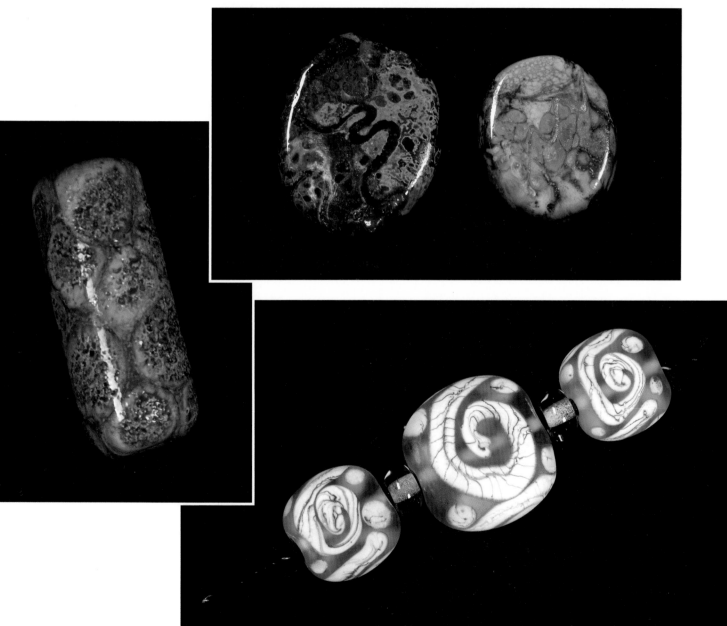

There are so many other techniques that you could spend the next decade exploring them. Here are some of my favorites, as well as others that I have yet to try.

Using any kind of frits can be hazardous to breathe, so always wear a respirator and have good ventilation when working with them.

Reduction frits have a very high metal content, and putting them in a propane-rich, reduction flame will bring that metal to the surface. The COE of reduction frits is not the same as that of Moretti glass, so it would seem wise to use them sparingly. I have rolled beads in them to get a heavy coating, and so far I've had no

problems, but be aware that problems could arise. Frits are available in different sized particles and many colors. Some of the things that can affect the final color of a reduction frit are the color of the base bead, the flame chemistry (too much or not enough propane), the temperature of the base bead, the humidity in the air, and the phase of the moon (just kidding on the last).

After rolling your bead in the frit and melting it in, it's very important to let the bead cool a little. Then turn up the propane or turn down the oxygen to get a reduction flame, and flash the bead quickly in and out of the flame. If it doesn't become metallic, try turning it in the flame closer to the torch or farther out, or try adding or reducing the amount of propane. The process can be reversed by putting the bead in a balanced or oxygen-rich flame. You can go back and forth, playing with the flame chemistry, but there is a limit, and the frit will eventually turn a dull gray. If it doesn't turn metallic quickly, it probably isn't going to work. Keep track of which frit and glass worked or didn't work, but be aware the results may be different on a different day. There are many variables involved, which is part of the fun of using reduction frits.

Kate Fowle Meleney, a beadmaker, worked with the Thompson Enamel Company to develop a set of enamels with the same COE as Moretti glass. Enamels are heavily pigmented ground glass, and these are produced in 80-mesh powder. Thirty-two colors are available, and you can mix them to create more colors. Rolling a bead in an enamel can be a great way to get just the right color on your bead, or you can add shading by sifting it on the bead, like the pink blush of color on a peach.

A great way to store the enamels is in watchmaker cases.

The melting temperature of these enamels is a little lower than that of Moretti glass, so use a slightly cooler flame when heating them. When placing enameled beads in the kiln, don't allow them to touch.

Breathing the dust from enamels can be hazardous, so wear a respirator and have good ventilation in your studio. Gently spoon rather than sprinkle the enamels whenever possible to avoid getting dust in the air.

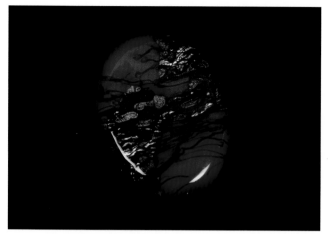

Silver foil and leaf, gold leaf, copper leaf, and palladium are the most commonly used metals by beadmakers. Foil is thicker than leaf and easier to handle. Most leaf is so thin it can't be touched and must be moved using tissue or a very soft brush. Typically a bead is heated and rolled on the metal foil or leaf. If the bead isn't warm enough, the metal won't stick. If it's too warm, it will lose its shape when you roll it. The metal leaf or foil can also be used to make a stringer, as done for the batik bead.

Gold is not reactive, and because of its expense, leaf is usually used rather than foil. It should also be burnished after applying it to the bead. The gold will burn off if the flame is too hot.

Copper leaf is reactive with many colors and needs a lot of heat to be absorbed into the glass. A light coating of an enamel can help this process. Apply a little enamel to your base bead, then the copper leaf.

Palladium is not reactive and can be heated repeatedly. By moving it in and out of the flame, you can create beautiful colors that resemble an oil slick.

Fine silver wire can be used to create trails of tiny silver balls. A thin wire 26-gauge or smaller works best. Melt one end of the wire onto the bead to attach it, wrap it around the bead, and burn off. Now hit the wire wrap with the flame, and it will melt into tiny balls. Wire conducts heat quickly, so be careful of your fingers.

Silver leaf or foil is very reactive with dark ivory and a few other colors. It should always be burnished, or rubbed, onto the glass. Too much heat will cause it to burn off.

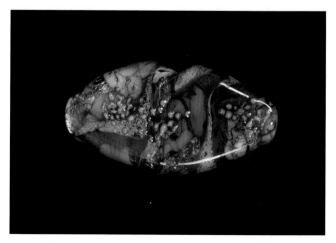

Some of my favorite beads are made using different combinations of enamels, silver and copper leaf, and reduction frits. Using two or more different metals on the same bead can produce unexpected results, so experiment.

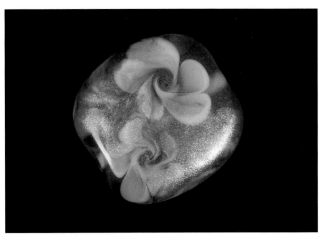

Pixie dust is powdered, colored mica, available in many colors and densities. Because it is so fine, it has a tendency to float all over your workspace.

If you want to add glass on top of the mica first, roll the bead on a wet cloth quickly to remove any loose mica. This will make it easier for the glass to stick. Also, transparent glass will stick to the mica easier than opaque colors.

Clean your tools after using pixie dust.

I store my pixie dust in large watchmaker cases. To use it, heat your base bead to a dull red, then roll it in the mica. The temperature of the bead is very important. If it's not hot enough, the mica won't stick. If it's too hot, the bead shape will be altered as you roll it. The mica burns and creates scum very easily, so it's usually added as the last step.

Dichroic glass has exotic colors created by a thin layer of metallic oxides on the surface. The base glass can be any color and texture, but clear and black are favorites of beadmakers. The dichroic layer looks one color in transmitted light and a complementary color in reflected light. This layer burns off easily, so keep it away from the flame as much as possible.

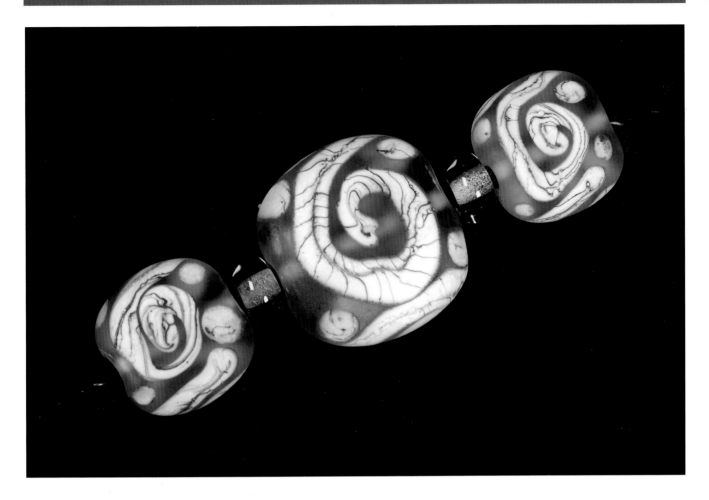

Etching glass results in a frosted or matte finish. When working with etching solutions, it's important to use eye and hand protection. Read and carefully follow the precautions on the bottle. Bifluoric acid is the usual ingredient today for etching soft glass, but it is not strong enough to etch borosilicate glass. Sandblasting or tumbling glass beads will result in a similar appearance to etching.

To etch beads, a liquid works well. Etching creams also work, although I think it's easier to get an even etch with a liquid. I use an old Pyrex measuring cup, which won't become etched by the solution. Place the beads in the cup, and carefully pour in enough etching solution to cover the beads. Follow the directions of the particular brand you are using, gently stir occasionally, and rinse well. If I want to etch just one or two beads, I string them on a monofilament cord and simply hang them in the bottle, following the directions for time.

To etch a design on the bead, mask off part of the glass to prevent those areas from being exposed to the solution. Several things can be used for this purpose. Commercial solutions are made for this use, but fingernail polish or white glue will also work. Let the mask dry before applying the etching solution. After rinsing off the solution, either dissolve the mask or peel it off.

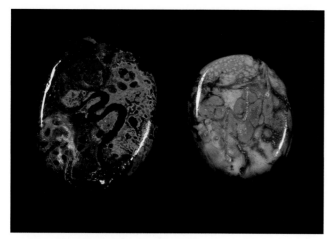

To add a little sparkle to your beads, try goldstone. This is actually copper suspended in glass, which must be compatible with the glass you are using for your bead.

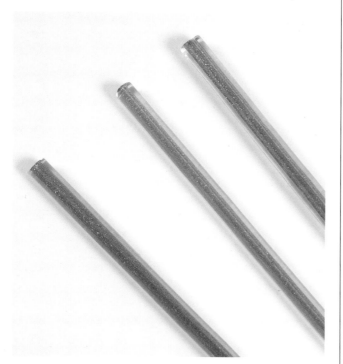

To use goldstone chips, heat the end of a clear rod and roll it in the chips. Gently melt them smooth, and then pull out stringers.

Chunks of goldstone shock easily, so heat them up first in your kiln. Then, using a clear rod as a punty, or handle, heat the tip and touch it to a chunk to pick it up. Then use another clear rod to cover the chunk completely. Now heat and pull out stringers.

Some goldstone has denser copper, resulting in more sparkle when it's pulled out into stringers. When buying chunks, look for ones with a dense gold color. You can pull stringers from goldstone rods, chips, or chunks. The sparkle in the goldstone will burn out if it is heated too much, so work it a little cooler than when pulling stringers from other glass.

When pulling goldstone rods into stringers, don't make them too thin or the copper will not be noticeable on your bead.

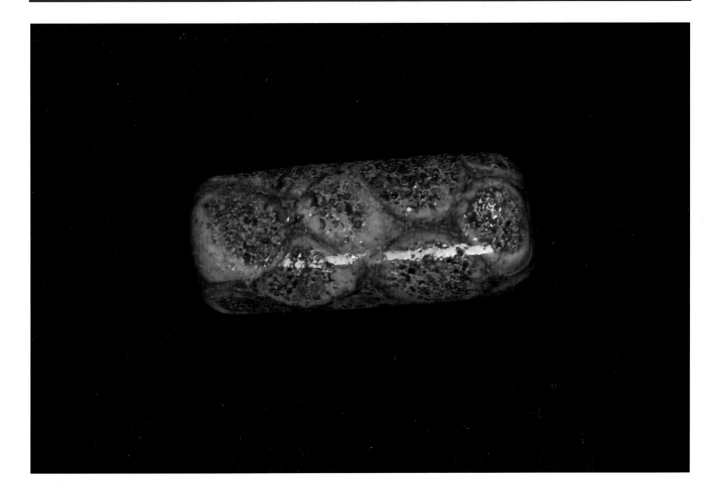

Rolling a bead in baking soda gives it a pitted surface, similar to that of a bead buried in the earth for hundreds of years. Make your bead, roll it in fresh baking soda, and return it to the flame, repeating as desired.

Keeping the bead in the flame longer will intensify the pitting, so experiment. After your bead is annealed and cool, wash it thoroughly or rinse it in vinegar to neutralize the baking soda.

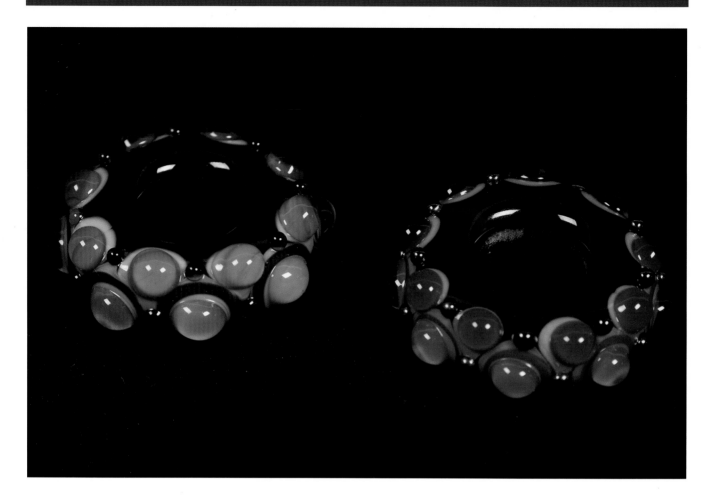

Sometimes you may want to use a mandrel that's larger or has a different shape. To make beads with large holes, you can use stainless steel tubing, available from any supplier, as a mandrel. After dipping it in bead release, blow the other end to blow out the dipped end, and let it dry before using it. Turning a tube can be tiring on your hands, and larger mandrels are a little easier to use. Different shaped mandrels that make the bead hole into a heart or cone are also available. When using these mandrels, the glass cools off faster than with a normal sized mandrel, so you must take care to keep the entire bead warm throughout the process.

If you want to make beads of the same size, there are several ways to do this. The easiest is simply to make a lot of beads and then match them in size. Sometimes I keep a bead the size I am trying to match on my bench so that I can quickly check it against the one I am working on.

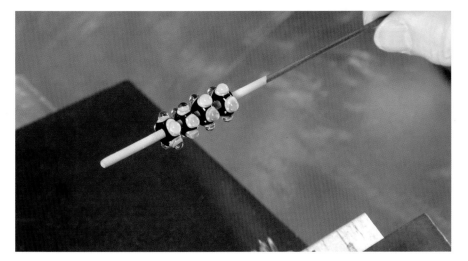

If the beads are small and not too elaborate, you can make two or more on the mandrel at the same time. When I started making multiple bubble beads with one row of dots, I made two at a time, and that worked well. Then I tried three and mastered that, and now I regularly make four at a time.

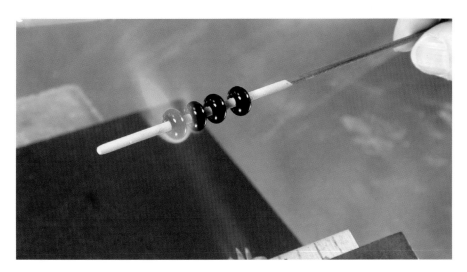

Starting close to your hand, and working out from there, make four small base beads about the same size, spaced about $^1/_4$ inch apart.

Then add a row of five dots around each bead. Begin with the bead closest to your hand, since that is the coolest.

You can't put one dot on each bead, then the second dot on each bead, and so on, because you won't get the spacing correct that way. Work quickly, and keep all the beads warm.

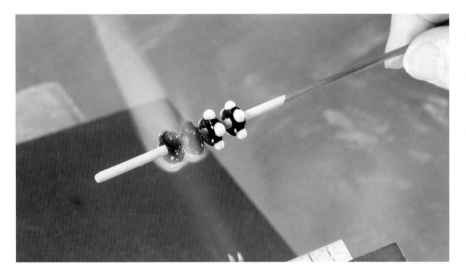

When all the dots are added, reheat all the beads, and then melt the dots smooth, starting with the one farthest from your hand. When those dots are almost melted, move to the next bead, keeping the mandrel turning at an even rate. The heat in the glass will continue to melt the dots on the first bead.

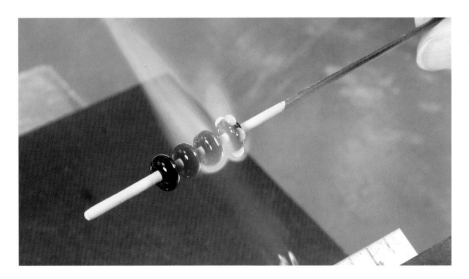

When the dots on the second bead are almost melted, move to the next bead and melt those dots.

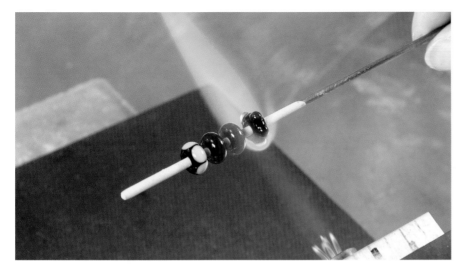

Continue this process until you finish the last bead, and then reheat all the beads. It's important to turn the mandrel at an even rate throughout this entire process to keep the beads from getting lopsided.

Once the dots are melted smooth and the beads are rigid, add raised dots starting with the bead farthest from your hand, which is the coolest bead at this point. Heat the rod of glass, touch it to the smooth dot, pull slightly, and then burn it off.

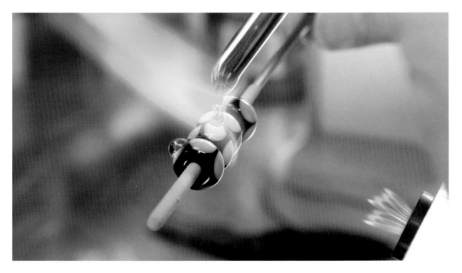

Add just one raised dot to the first bead, then one to the second, then the third and fourth.

Now put the second raised dot on the fourth bead first and work back to the first bead, and continue back and forth until all the raised dots are added. Turn the mandrel slightly so that the dots are not added in a straight line; this helps keep them from overheating and melting too much. Also keep the flame slightly pointed in the direction you are working, away from the dot you just added.

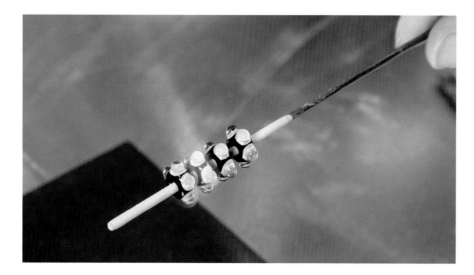

To finish, flame anneal the beads, and then put them in the kiln to be annealed.

The timing is crucial. With practice, you will develop an internal clock to know how long the bead can cool before it needs to be reheated. Making several beads at a time will help this along.

SUPPLIES AND RESOURCES

LAMPWORKING MATERIALS AND EQUIPMENT

Arrow Springs
4301 A Product Drive
Shingle Springs, CA 95682
(800) 899-0689
ArrowSprings.com

Frantz Art Glass and Supply
130 W. Corporate Rd.
Shelton, WA 98584
(360) 426-6712
(800) 839-6712
FrantzArtGlass.com
FrantzNewsletter.com

Wale Apparatus Co.
400 Front St.
P.O. Box D
Hellertown, PA 18055
(610) 838-7047
(800) 334-9253
waleapparatus.com

RESOURCES

The Bead Museum, on the ground floor of the Jenifer Building, 400 Seventh St. NW, Washington, DC 20004, was founded by the Bead Society of Greater Washington in 1995 and opened in 1997. The museum hosts changing exhibitions and has a permanent bead timeline exhibit. More information can be found at www.beadmuseumdc.org.

The International Society of Glass Beadmakers maintains a website at www.isgb.org. A wealth of information is available there, along with an active forum for posting questions and sharing information. There are many bead societies in existence, each with their own emphasis. A search on the Internet or a look through current bead magazines may help you find a society near you.

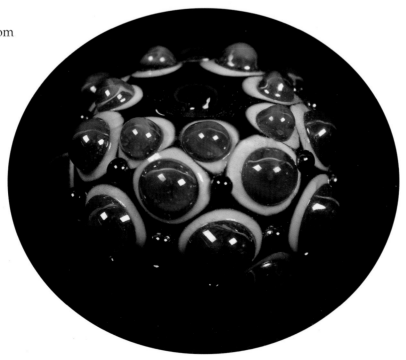

BIBLIOGRAPHY

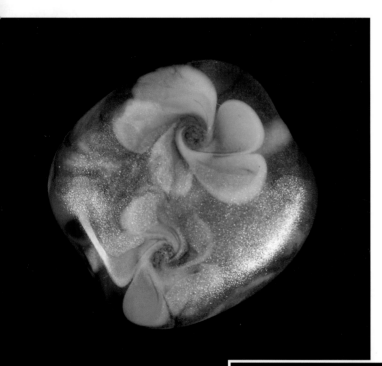

Dubin, Lois Sherr. *The History of Beads*. New York: Harry N. Abrams, 1995.

Dunham, Bandhu Scott. *Contemporary Lampworking*. Prescott, AZ: Salusa Glassworks, 1997.

Kervin, James. *More Than You Ever Wanted to Know about Glass Beadmaking*. Livermore, CA: GlassWear Studios, 1996.

Lankton, James W. *A Bead Timeline*. Vol. 1, *Prehistory to 1200 CE*. Washington DC: Bead Society of Greater Washington, 2003.

Liu, Robert K. *Collectible Beads: A Universal Aesthetic*. Vista, CA: Ornament, 1995

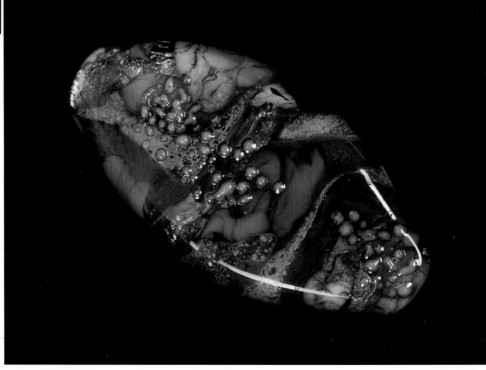